T5-CQF-771

Liturgy
Documentary
Series 4

Christian
Initiation of
Adults

Revised

ISBN 1-55586-895-9

Excerpts from the English translation of and pastoral notes from the *Rite of Christian Initiation of Adults,* © 1986 International Committee on English in the Liturgy, Inc., Washington, D.C.

Contents

FOREWORD

In 1972 when the *Ordo Initiationis Christianae Adultorum* was promulgated by the Holy See, the Church was given a wholly new ritual to celebrate and mark the stages of Christian conversion and rebirth. For the first time since the patristic age, the Latin West possessed rites of initiation for adults that were not merely the rearrangement or evolution of baptismal rites for children. Since 1972, and particularly since 1974 when the *Rite of Christian Initiation of Adults* was first made available in the English language, the Church's mission of evangelization and catechesis has been transformed both by the theology of Christian initiation and the structure and processes of the new ritual.

Promulgated on 6 January 1972 by Decree of the Congregation for Divine Worship (Prot. 15/72) when Cardinal Tabera was Prefect and Archbishop Annibale Bugnini was Secretary, the catechumenate and its rites were fully restored, in keeping with the mandate of the Second Vatican Council:

> The catechumenate for adults, divided into several stages, is to be restored and put into use at the discretion of the local Ordinary. By this means the time of the catechumenate, which is intended as a period of well-suited instruction, may be sanctified by sacred rites to be celebrated at successive intervals of time (*Sacrosanctum Concilium* 64; see also 65, 66, 69).

A provisional translation was prepared by the International Commission on English in the Liturgy in 1974 and approved for use in the dioceses of the United States of America by the Executive Committee of the National Conference of Catholic Bishops. When confirmed by the Congregation for Divine Worship on 23 September 1974 (Prot. 1993/74), the *Rite of Christian Initiation of Adults* was published by the United States Catholic Conference for immediate use in the United States.

While the new rites initially seemed strange and even archaic to some people, the catechumenate was slowly restored in the United States, taking the place of individual "convert instructions." The influence of the *Rite of Christian Initiation of Adults* was felt also in those situations in which baptized Christians of other churches were being received into full communion with the Catholic Church, as well as in programs and processes devised to receive once again into the full and active life of the Church those Catholics who, for various reasons, never practiced or lived their faith. In

1

short, the "catechumenal process" and the sound theological and anthropological framework of the *Rite of Christian Initiation of Adults* have given new life to various movements and ministries in the life of the Church.

The final translation or "White Book" of the *Rite of Christian Initiation of Adults* was prepared by the International Commission on English in the Liturgy and made available to the member and associate member conferences of the Joint Commission in January of 1986. This new edition of the *Rite of Christian Initiation of Adults* was confirmed by the Apostolic See on 19 February 1988. Its use is mandatory as of 1 September 1988.

This new *Rite of Christian Initiation of Adults* differs in several ways from the previous edition. The introduction of the rite has been reworked and parts of it have been redistributed to the appropriate sections of the book. New rites for use with the already baptized have been prepared for use in the United States as well as combined rites for use when there are both catechumens and candidates for reception and/or confirmation and eucharist.

This volume of the *Liturgy Documentary Series* will prove to be of benefit not only to liturgists and students of ritual, but also to those engaged in the mission and ministry of evangelization and catechesis.

Reverend John A. Gurrieri
Executive Director
Secretariat
Bishops' Committee on the Liturgy
National Conference of Catholic Bishops

Editor's Note:

The editorial rearrangement omits nothing from the Latin original, but it does entail a departure from the paragraph enumeration of the Latin edition. For each paragraph of the English edition bearing the number proper to this edition, the right-hand margin carries the reference number or numbers indicating the corresponding paragraph or paragraphs of the Latin edition. A reference number in the right-hand margin that is preceded by a letter indicates a text from a source other than the *Ordo initiationis christianae adultorum*; numbers that are preceded by the letters "RM" refer to *The*

Roman Missal; numbers that are preceded by the letters "PC" refer to *Pastoral Care of the Sick: Rites of Anointing and Viaticum*; numbers preceded by "R" refer to the appendix of the *Ordo initiationis*, "Rite of Reception of Baptized Christians into the Full Communion of the Catholic Church"; and numbers preceded by "P" refer to the *Rite of Penance*. Rites and texts prepared specifically for use in the dioceses of the United States of America are designated "USA" in the margin.

THE ROMAN RITUAL

CHRISTIAN
INITIATION

CHRISTIAN INITIATION
GENERAL INTRODUCTION

1   In the sacraments of Christian initiation we are freed from the power of darkness and joined to Christ's death, burial, and resurrection. We receive the Spirit of filial adoption and are part of the entire people of God in the celebration of the memorial of the Lord's death and resurrection.[1]

2   Baptism incorporates us into Christ and forms us into God's people. This first sacrament pardons all our sins, rescues us from the power of darkness, and brings us to the dignity of adopted children,[2] a new creation through water and the Holy Spirit. Hence we are called and are indeed the children of God.[3]

By signing us with the gift of the Spirit, confirmation makes us more completely the image of the Lord and fills us with the Holy Spirit, so that we may bear witness to him before all the world and work to bring the Body of Christ to its fullness as soon as possible.[4]

Finally, coming to the table of the eucharist, we eat the flesh and drink the blood of the Son of Man so that we may have eternal life[5] and show forth the unity of God's people. By offering ourselves with Christ, we share in the universal sacrifice, that is, the entire community of the redeemed offered to God by their High Priest,[6] and we pray for a greater outpouring of the Holy Spirit, so that the whole human race may be brought into the unity of God's family.[7]

Thus the three sacraments of Christian initiation closely combine to bring us, the faithful of Christ, to his full stature and to enable us to carry out the mission of the entire people of God in the Church and in the world.[8]

---

[1] See Vatican Council II, Decree on the Church's Missionary Activity *Ad gentes*, no. 14.

[2] See Colossians 1:13; Romans 8:15; Galatians 4:5. See also Council of Trent, sess. 6, *Decr. de justificatione*, cap. 4: Denz.-Schön. 1524.

[3] See 1 John 3:1.

[4] See Vatican Council II, Decree on the Church's Missionary Activity *Ad gentes*, no. 36.

[5] See John 6:55.

[6] See Augustine, *De civitate Dei* 10,6: PL 41, 284. Vatican Council II, Dogmatic Constitution on the Church *Lumen gentium*, no. 11; Decree on the Ministry and Life of Priests *Presbyterorum Ordinis*, no. 2.

[7] See Vatican Council II, Dogmatic Constitution on the Church *Lumen gentium*, no. 28.

[8] See ibid., no. 31.

3   Baptism, the door to life and to the kingdom of God, is the first sacrament of the New Law, which Christ offered to all, that they might have eternal life.[9] He later entrusted this sacrament and the Gospel to his Church, when he told his apostles: "Go, make disciples of all nations, and baptize them in the name of the Father, and of the Son, and of the Holy Spirit."[10] Baptism is therefore, above all, the sacrament of that faith by which, enlightened by the grace of the Holy Spirit, we respond to the Gospel of Christ. That is why the Church believes that it is its most basic and necessary duty to inspire all, catechumens, parents of children still to be baptized, and godparents, to that true and living faith by which they hold fast to Christ and enter into or confirm their commitment to the New Covenant. In order to enliven such faith, the Church prescribes the pastoral instruction of catechumens, the preparation of the children's parents, the celebration of God's word, and the profession of faith at the celebration of baptism.

4   Further, baptism is the sacrament by which its recipients are incorporated into the Church and are built up together in the Spirit into a house where God lives,[11] into a holy nation and a royal priesthood.[12] Baptism is a sacramental bond of unity linking all who have been signed by it.[13] Because of that unchangeable effect (given expression in the Latin liturgy by the anointing of the baptized person with chrism in the presence of God's people), the rite of baptism is held in highest honor by all Christians. Once it has been validly celebrated, even if by Christians with whom we are not in full communion, it may never lawfully be repeated.

5   Baptism, the cleansing with water by the power of the living word,[14] washes away every stain of sin, original and personal, makes us sharers in God's own life[15] and his adopted children.[16] As proclaimed in the prayers

---

[9] See John 3:5.

[10] Matthew 28:19.

[11] See Ephesians 2:22.

[12] See 1 Peter 2:9.

[13] See Vatican Council II, Decree on Ecumenism *Unitatis redintegratio,* no. 22.

[14] See Ephesians 5:26.

[15] See 2 Peter 1:4.

[16] See Romans 8:15; Galatians 4:5.

for the blessing of the water, baptism is a cleansing water of rebirth[17] that makes us God's children born from on high. The blessed Trinity is invoked over those who are to be baptized, so that all who are signed in this name are consecrated to the Trinity and enter into communion with the Father, the Son, and the Holy Spirit. They are prepared for this high dignity and led to it by the scriptural readings, the prayer of the community, and their own profession of belief in the Father, the Son, and the Holy Spirit.

6   Far superior to the purifications of the Old Law, baptism produces these effects by the power of the mystery of the Lord's passion and resurrection. Those who are baptized are united to Christ in a death like his;[18] buried with him in death, they are given life again with him, and with him they rise again.[19] For baptism recalls and makes present the paschal mystery itself, because in baptism we pass from the death of sin into life. The celebration of baptism should therefore reflect the joy of the resurrection, especially when the celebration takes place during the Easter Vigil or on a Sunday.

OFFICES AND MINISTRIES OF BAPTISM

7   The preparation for baptism and Christian instruction are both of vital concern to God's people, the Church, which hands on and nourishes the faith received from the apostles. Through the ministry of the Church, adults are called to the Gospel by the Holy Spirit and infants are baptized in the faith of the Church and brought up in that faith. Therefore it is most important that catechists and other laypersons should work with priests and deacons in the preparation for baptism. In the actual celebration, the people of God (represented not only by the parents, godparents, and relatives, but also, as far as possible, by friends, neighbors, and some members of the local Church) should take an active part. Thus they will show their common faith and the shared joy with which the newly baptized are received into the community of the Church.

8   It is a very ancient custom of the Church that adults are not admitted to baptism without godparents, members of the Christian community who

---

[17] See Titus 3:5.

[18] See Romans 6:4-5.

[19] See Ephesians 2:5-6.

will assist the candidates at least in the final preparation for baptism and after baptism will help them persevere in the faith and in their lives as Christians. In the baptism of children, as well, godparents are to be present in order to represent both the expanded spiritual family of the one to be baptized and the role of the Church as a mother. As occasion offers, godparents help the parents so that children will come to profess the faith and live up to it.

9   At least in the later rites of the catechumenate and in the actual celebration of baptism, the part of godparents is to testify to the faith of adult candidates or, together with the parents, to profess the Church's faith, in which children are baptized.

10   Therefore godparents, chosen by the catechumens or by the families of children to be baptized, must, in the judgment of the parish priest (pastor), be qualified to carry out the proper liturgical functions mentioned in no. 9.

1. Godparents are persons, other than the parents of candidates, who are designated by the candidates themselves or by a candidate's parents or whoever stands in the place of parents, or, in the absence of these, by the parish priest (pastor) or the minister of baptism. Each candidate may have either a godmother or a godfather or both a godmother and a godfather.

2. Those designated must have the capability and intention of carrying out the responsibility of a godparent and be mature enough to do so. A person sixteen years of age is presumed to have the requisite maturity, but the diocesan bishop may have stipulated another age or the parish priest (pastor) or the minister may decide that there is a legitimate reason for allowing an exception.

3. Those designated as godparents must have received the three sacraments of initiation, baptism, confirmation, and eucharist, and be living a life consistent with faith and with the responsibility of a godparent.

4. Those designated as godparents must also be members of the Catholic Church and be canonically free to carry out this office. At the request of parents, a baptized and believing Christian not belonging to the Catholic Church may act as a Christian witness along with a Catholic godparent.[20]

---

[20] See *Codex Iuris Canonici,* can. 873 and 874, §§ 1 and 2.

In the case of separated Eastern Christians with whom we do not have full communion the special discipline for the Eastern Churches is to be respected.

11 The ordinary ministers of baptism are bishops, priests, and deacons.

1. In every celebration of this sacrament they should be mindful that they act in the Church in the name of Christ and by the power of the Holy Spirit.

2. They should therefore be diligent in the ministry of the word of God and in the manner of celebrating the sacrament. They must avoid any action that the faithful could rightly regard as favoritism.[21]

3. Except in a case of necessity, these ministers are not to confer baptism outside their own territory, even on their own subjects, without the requisite permission.

12 Bishops are the chief stewards of the mysteries of God and leaders of the entire liturgical life in the Church committed to them.[22] This is why they direct the conferring of baptism, which brings to the recipient a share in the kingly priesthood of Christ.[23] Therefore bishops should personally celebrate baptism, especially at the Easter Vigil. They should have a particular concern for the preparation and baptism of adults.

13 It is the duty of parish priests (pastors) to assist the bishop in the instruction and baptism of the adults entrusted to their care, unless the bishop makes other provisions. Parish priests (pastors), with the assistance of catechists or other qualified laypersons, have the duty of preparing the parents and godparents of children through appropriate pastoral guidance and of baptizing the children.

14 Other priests and deacons, since they are co-workers in the ministry of bishops and parish priests (pastors), also prepare candidates for baptism and,

---

[21] See Vatican Council II, Constitution on the Liturgy *Sacrosanctum Concilium*, art. 32; Pastoral Constitution on the Church in the Modern World *Gaudium et spes*, no. 29.

[22] See Vatican Council II, Decree on the Pastoral Office of Bishops *Christus Dominus*, no. 15.

[23] See Vatican Council II, Dogmatic Constitution on the Church *Lumen gentium*, no. 26.

by the invitation or consent of the bishop or parish priest (pastor), celebrate the sacrament.

15   The celebrant of baptism may be assisted by other priests and deacons and also by laypersons in those parts that pertain to them, especially if there are a large number to be baptized. Provision for this is made in various parts of the rituals for adults and for children.

16   In imminent danger of death and especially at the moment of death, when no priest or deacon is available, any member of the faithful, indeed anyone with the right intention, may and sometimes must administer baptism. In a case simply of danger of death the sacrament should be administered, if possible, by a member of the faithful according to one of the shorter rites provided by this situation.[24] Even in this case a small community should be formed to assist at the rite or, if possible, at least one or two witnesses should be present.

17   Since they belong to the priestly people, all laypersons, especially parents and, by reason of their work, catechists, midwives, family or social workers or nurses of the sick, as well as physicians and surgeons, should be thoroughly aware, according to their capacities, of the proper method of baptizing in case of emergency. They should be taught by parish priests (pastors), deacons, and catechists. Bishops should provide appropriate means within their diocese for such instruction.

REQUIREMENTS FOR THE CELEBRATION OF BAPTISM

18   The water used in baptism should be true water and, both for the sake of authentic sacramental symbolism and for hygienic reasons, should be pure and clean.

19   The baptismal font, or the vessel in which on occasion the water is prepared for celebration of the sacrament in the sanctuary, should be spotlessly clean and of pleasing design.

---

[24] See *Rite of Christian Initiation of Adults,* nos. 375-399; *Rite of Baptism for Children,* nos. 157-164.

20   If the climate requires, provision should be made for the water to be heated beforehand.

21   Except in case of necessity, a priest or deacon is to use only water that has been blessed for the rite. The water blessed at the Easter Vigil should, if possible, be kept and used throughout the Easter season to signify more clearly the relationship between the sacrament of baptism and the paschal mystery. Outside the Easter season, it is desirable that the water be blessed for each occasion, in order that the words of blessing may explicitly express the mystery of salvation that the Church remembers and proclaims. If the baptistery is supplied with running water, the blessing is given as the water flows.

22   As the rite for baptizing, either immersion, which is more suitable as a symbol of participation in the death and resurrection of Christ, or pouring may lawfully be used.

23   The words for conferring baptism in the Latin Church are: I BAPTIZE YOU IN THE NAME OF THE FATHER, AND OF THE SON, AND OF THE HOLY SPIRIT.

24   For celebrating the liturgy of the word of God a suitable place should be provided in the baptistery or in the church.

25   The baptistery or the area where the baptismal font is located should be reserved for the sacrament of baptism and should be worthy to serve as the place where Christians are reborn in water and the Holy Spirit. The baptistery may be situated in a chapel either inside or outside the church or in some other part of the church easily seen by the faithful; it should be large enough to accommodate a good number of people. After the Easter season, the Easter candle should be kept reverently in the baptistery, in such a way that it can be lighted for the celebration of baptism and so that from it the candles for the newly baptized can easily be lighted.

26   In the celebration the parts of the rite that are to be celebrated outside the baptistery should be carried out in different areas of the church that most conveniently suit the size of the congregation and the several parts of the baptismal liturgy. When the baptistery cannot accommodate all the catechumens and the congregation, the parts of the rite that are customarily

celebrated inside the baptistery may be transferred to some other suitable area of the church.

27   As far as possible, all recently born babies should be baptized at a common celebration on the same day. Except for a good reason, baptism should not be celebrated more than once on the same day in the same church.

28   Further details concerning the time for baptism of adults and of children will be found in the respective rituals. But at all times the celebration of the sacrament should have a markedly paschal character.

29   Parish priests (pastors) must carefully and without delay record in the baptismal register the names of those baptized, of the minister, parents, and godparents, as well as the place and date of baptism.

ADAPTATIONS BY THE CONFERENCES OF BISHOPS

30   According to the Constitution of the Liturgy (art. 63, b), it is within the competence of the conferences of bishops to compose for their local rituals a section corresponding to this one in the Roman Ritual, adapted to the needs of their respective regions. After it has been reviewed by the Apostolic See, it may be used in the regions for which it was prepared.
   In this connection, it is the responsibility of each conference of bishops:

1. to decide on the adaptations mentioned in the Constitution on the Liturgy (art. 39);

2. carefully and prudently to weigh what elements of a people's distinctive traditions and culture may suitably be admitted into divine worship and so to propose to the Apostolic See other adaptations considered useful or necessary that will be introduced with its consent;

3. to retain distinctive elements of any existing local rituals, as long as they conform to the Constitution on the Liturgy and correspond to contemporary needs, or to modify such elements;

4. to prepare translations of the texts that genuinely reflect the charac-

teristics of various languages and cultures and to add, whenever helpful, music suitable for singing;

5. to adapt and augment the Introductions contained in the Roman Ritual, so that the ministers may fully understand the meaning of the rites and carry them out effectively;

6. to arrange the material in the various editions of the liturgical books prepared under the guidance of the conference of bishops, so that these books may better suit pastoral use.

31   Taking into consideration especially the norms in the Constitution on the Liturgy (art. 37-40, 65), the conferences of bishops in mission countries have the responsibility of judging whether the elements of initiation in use among some peoples can be adapted for the rite of Christian baptism and of deciding whether such elements are to be incorporated into the rite.

32   When the Roman Ritual for baptism provides several optional formularies, local rituals may add other formularies of the same kind.

33   The celebration of baptism is greatly enhanced by the use of song, which stimulates in the participants a sense of their unity, fosters their praying together, and expresses the joy of Easter that should permeate the whole rite. The conference of bishops should therefore encourage and help specialists in music to compose settings for those liturgical texts particularly suited to congregational singing.

ADAPTATIONS BY THE MINISTER OF BAPTISM

34   Taking into account existing circumstances and other needs, as well as the wishes of the faithful, the minister should make full use of the various options allowed in the rite.

35   In addition to the adaptations that are provided in the Roman Ritual for the dialogue and blessings, the minister may make other adaptations for special circumstances. These adaptations will be indicated more fully in the Introductions to the rites of baptism for adults and for children.

THE ROMAN RITUAL
REVISED BY DECREE OF THE SECOND VATICAN ECUMENICAL COUNCIL AND PUBLISHED BY AUTHORITY OF POPE PAUL VI

RITE OF
CHRISTIAN INITIATION
OF ADULTS
APPROVED FOR USE IN THE DIOCESES OF THE UNITED STATES OF
AMERICA BY THE NATIONAL CONFERENCE OF CATHOLIC BISHOPS
AND CONFIRMED BY THE APOSTOLIC SEE

CONGREGATION FOR DIVINE WORSHIP

Prot. no. 15/72

DECREE

The Second Vatican Council prescribed the revision of the rite of baptism of adults and decreed that the catechumenate for adults, divided into several steps, should be restored. By this means the time of the catechumenate, which is intended as a period of well-suited instruction, would be sanctified by liturgical rites to be celebrated at successive intervals of time. The Council likewise decreed that both the solemn and simple rites of adult baptism should be revised, with proper attention to the restored catechumenate.

In observance of these decrees, the Congregation for Divine Worship prepared a new rite for the Christian initiation of adults, which Pope Paul VI has approved. The Congregation now publishes it and declares the present edition to be the *editio typica*, to replace the rite of baptism of adults now in the Roman Ritual. It likewise decrees that this new rite may be used in Latin at once and in the vernacular from the day appointed by the conference of bishops, after it has prepared a translation and had it confirmed by the Apostolic See.

All things to the contrary notwithstanding.

From the office of the Congregation for Divine Worship, 6 January 1972, Epiphany.

Arturo Cardinal Tabera
Prefect

A. Bugnini
Secretary

NATIONAL CONFERENCE OF CATHOLIC BISHOPS, UNITED STATES OF AMERICA

DECREE

In accord with the norms established by decree of the Sacred Congregation of Rites in *Cum, nostra aetate* (27 January 1966), this edition of the *Rite of Christian Initiation of Adults* is declared to be the vernacular typical edition of *Ordo initiationis christianae adultorum* in the dioceses of the United States of America, and is published by authority of the National Conference of Catholic Bishops.

The *Rite of Christian Initiation of Adults* was canonically approved by the National Conference of Catholic Bishops in plenary assembly on 11 November 1986 and was subsequently confirmed by the Apostolic See by decree of the Congregation for Divine Worship on 19 February 1988 (Prot. N. 1192/86).

On 1 July 1988 the *Rite of Christian Initiation of Adults* may be published and used in the liturgy. From 1 September 1988 the use of the *Rite of Christian Initiation of Adults* is mandatory in the dioceses of the United States of America. From that day forward no other English version may be used.

Given at the General Secretariat of the National Conference of Catholic Bishops, Washington, D.C., on 18 March 1988, the memorial of Saint Cyril of Jerusalem, bishop and doctor of the Church.

+ John L. May
Archbishop of Saint Louis
President
National Conference of Catholic Bishops

Daniel F. Hoye
General Secretary

INTRODUCTION

1   The rite of Christian initiation presented here is designed for adults who, 1
after hearing the mystery of Christ proclaimed, consciously and freely seek
the living God and enter the way of faith and conversion as the Holy Spirit
opens their hearts. By God's help they will be strengthened spiritually during
their preparation and at the proper time will receive the sacraments fruitfully.

2   This rite includes not simply the celebration of the sacraments of baptism, 2
confirmation, and eucharist, but also all the rites belonging to the catechumenate. Endorsed by the ancient practice of the Church, a catechumenate
that would be suited to contemporary missionary activity in all regions was
so widely requested that the Second Vatican Council decreed its restoration,
revision, and adaptation to local traditions.[1]

3   So that the rite of initiation will be more useful for the work of the Church 3
and for individual, parochial, and missionary circumstances, the rite is first
presented in Part I of this book in its complete and usual form (nos. 36–
251). This is designed for the preparation of a group of candidates, but by
simple adaptation pastors can devise a form suited to one person.

Part II provides rites for special circumstances: the Christian initiation of
children (nos. 252–330), a simple form of the rite for adults to be carried
out in exceptional circumstances (nos. 331–369), and a short form of the
rite for those in danger of death (nos. 370–399). Part II also includes guidelines for preparing uncatechized adults for confirmation and eucharist (nos.
400–410) along with four (4) optional rites which may be used with such
candidates, and the rite of reception of baptized Christians into the full
communion of the Catholic Church (nos. 473–504).

Rites for catechumens and baptized but previously uncatechized adults
celebrated in combination, along with a rite combining the reception of
baptized Christians into the full communion of the Catholic Church with
the celebration of Christian initiation at the Easter Vigil (nos. 562–594), are
contained in Appendix I. The two additional appendices contain acclama-

---

[1] See Vatican Council II, Constitution on the Liturgy *Sacrosanctum Concilium,* art. 64-66;
Decree on the Church's Missionary Activity *Ad gentes,* no. 14; Decree on the Pastoral Office
of Bishops *Christus Dominus,* no. 14.

tions, hymns, and songs, and the National Statutes for the Catechumenate in the Dioceses of the United States of America.

STRUCTURE OF THE INITIATION OF ADULTS

4   The initiation of catechumens is a gradual process that takes place within the community of the faithful. By joining the catechumens in reflecting on the value of the paschal mystery and by renewing their own conversion, the faithful provide an example that will help the catechumens to obey the Holy Spirit more generously.

5   The rite of initiation is suited to a spiritual journey of adults that varies according to the many forms of God's grace, the free cooperation of the individuals, the action of the Church, and the circumstances of time and place.

6   This journey includes not only the periods for making inquiry and for maturing (see no. 7), but also the steps marking the catechumens' progress, as they pass, so to speak, through another doorway or ascend to the next level.

1. The first step: reaching the point of initial conversion and wishing to become Christians, they are accepted as catechumens by the Church.

2. The second step: having progressed in faith and nearly completed the catechumenate, they are accepted into a more intense preparation for the sacraments of initiation.

3. The third step: having completed their spiritual preparation, they receive the sacraments of Christian initiation.

These three steps are to be regarded as the major, more intense moments of initiation and are marked by three liturgical rites: the first by the rite of acceptance into the order of catechumens (nos. 41–74); the second by the rite of election or enrollment of names (nos. 118–137); and the third by the celebration of the sacraments of Christian initiation (nos. 206–243).

7   The steps lead to periods of inquiry and growth; alternatively the periods may also be seen as preparing for the ensuing step.

1. The first period consists of inquiry on the part of the candidates and of evangelization and the precatechumenate on the part of the Church. It ends with the rite of acceptance into the order of catechumens.

2. The second period, which begins with the rite of acceptance into the order of catechumens and may last for several years, includes catechesis and the rites connected with catechesis. It comes to an end on the day of election.

3. The third and much shorter period, which follows the rite of election, ordinarily coincides with the Lenten preparation for the Easter celebration and the sacraments of initiation. It is a time of purification and enlightenment and includes the celebration of the rites belonging to this period.

4. The final period extends through the whole Easter season and is devoted to the postbaptismal catechesis or mystagogy. It is a time for deepening the Christian experience, for spiritual growth, and for entering more fully into the life and unity of the community.

Thus there are four continuous periods: the precatechumenate, the period for hearing the first preaching of the Gospel (nos. 36–40); the period of the catechumenate, set aside for a thorough catechesis and for the rites belonging to this period (nos. 75–117); the period of purification and enlightenment (Lenten preparation), designed for a more intense spiritual preparation, which is assisted by the celebration of the scrutinies and presentations (nos. 138–205); and the period of postbaptismal catechesis or mystagogy, marked by the new experience of sacraments and community (nos. 224–251).

8 The whole initiation must bear a markedly paschal character, since the initiation of Christians is the first sacramental sharing in Christ's dying and rising and since, in addition, the period of purification and enlightenment ordinarily coincides with Lent[2] and the period of postbaptismal catechesis or mystagogy with the Easter season. All the resources of Lent should be brought to bear as a more intense preparation of the elect and the Easter Vigil should be regarded as the proper time for the sacraments of initiation. Because of pastoral needs, however, the sacraments of initiation may be celebrated at other times (see nos. 26–30).

8

---

[2] See Vatican Council II, Constitution on the Liturgy *Sacrosanctum Concilium*, art. 109.

MINISTRIES AND OFFICES

9   In light of what is said in *Christian Initiation,* General Introduction (no. 7), the people of God, as represented by the local Church, should understand and show by their concern that the initiation of adults is the responsibility of all the baptized.[3] Therefore the community must always be fully prepared in the pursuit of its apostolic vocation to give help to those who are searching for Christ. In the various circumstances of daily life, even as in the apostolate, all the followers of Christ have the obligation of spreading the faith according to their abilities.[4] Hence, the entire community must help the candidates and the catechumens throughout the process of initiation: during the period of the precatechumenate, the period of the catechumenate, the period of purification and enlightenment, and the period of postbaptismal catechesis or mystagogy. In particular:

1. During the period of evangelization and precatechumenate, the faithful should remember that for the Church and its members the supreme purpose of the apostolate is that Christ's message is made known to the world by word and deed and that his grace is communicated.[5] They should therefore show themselves ready to give the candidates evidence of the spirit of the Christian community and to welcome them into their homes, into personal conversation, and into community gatherings.

2. At the celebrations belonging to the period of the catechumenate, the faithful should seek to be present whenever possible and should take an active part in the responses, prayers, singing, and acclamations.

3. On the day of election, because it is a day of growth for the community, the faithful, when called upon, should be sure to give honest and carefully considered testimony about the catechumens.

4. During Lent, the period of purification and enlightenment, the faithful should take care to participate in the rites of the scrutinies and presentations and give the elect the example of their own renewal in the spirit

---

[3] See Vatican Council II, Decree on the Church's Missionary Activity *Ad gentes,* no. 14.
[4] See Vatican Council II, Dogmatic Constitution on the Church *Lumen gentium,* no. 17.
[5] See Vatican Council II, Decree on the Apostolate of the Laity *Apostolicam actuositatem* no. 6.

of penance, faith, and charity. At the Easter Vigil, they should attach great importance to renewing their own baptismal promises.

5. During the period immediately after baptism, the faithful should take part in the Masses for neophytes, that is, the Sunday Masses of the Easter season (see no. 25), welcome the neophytes with open arms in charity, and help them to feel more at home in the community of the baptized.

10   A sponsor accompanies any candidate seeking admission as a catechu- 42
men. Sponsors are persons who have known and assisted the candidates and stand as witnesses to the candidates' moral character, faith, and intention. It may happen that it is not the sponsor for the rite of acceptance and the period of the catechumenate but another person who serves as godparent for the periods of purification and enlightenment and of mystagogy.

11   Their godparents (for each a godmother or godfather, or both) accom- 43
pany the candidates on the day of election, at the celebration of the sacraments of initiation, and during the period of mystagogy.[6] Godparents are persons chosen by the candidates on the basis of example, good qualities, and friendship, delegated by the local Christian community, and approved by the priest. It is the responsibility of godparents to show the candidates how to practice the Gospel in personal and social life, to sustain the candidates in moments of hesitancy and anxiety, to bear witness, and to guide the candidates' progress in the baptismal life. Chosen before the candidates' election, godparents fulfill this office publicly from the day of the rite of election, when they give testimony to the community about the candidates. They continue to be important during the time after reception of the sacraments when the neophytes need to be assisted so that they remain true to their baptismal promises.

12   The bishop,[7] in person or through his delegate, sets up, regulates, and 44
promotes the program of pastoral formation for catechumens and admits the candidates to their election and to the sacraments. It is hoped that, presiding if possible at the Lenten liturgy, he will himself celebrate the rite of election and, at the Easter Vigil, the sacraments of initiation, at least for the initiation

---

[6] See *Christian Initiation,* General Introduction, nos. 8 and 10.1.
[7] See ibid., no. 12.

of those who are fourteen years old or older. Finally, when pastoral care requires, the bishop should depute catechists, truly worthy and properly prepared, to celebrate the minor exorcisms (nos. 90–94) and the blessings of the catechumens (nos. 95–97).

13   Priests, in addition to their usual ministry for any celebration of baptism, confirmation, and the eucharist,[8] have the responsibility of attending to the pastoral and personal care of the catechumens,[9] especially those who seem hesitant and discouraged. With the help of deacons and catechists, they are to provide instruction for the catechumens; they are also to approve the choice of godparents and willingly listen to and help them; they are to be diligent in the correct celebration and adaptation of the rites throughout the entire course of Christian initiation (see no. 35).

14   The priest who baptizes an adult or a child of catechetical age should, when the bishop is absent, also confer confirmation,[10] unless this sacrament is to be given at another time (see no. 24). When there are a large number of candidates to be confirmed, the minister of confirmation may associate priests with himself to administer the sacrament. It is preferable that the priests who are so invited:

1. either have a particular function or office in the diocese, being, namely, either vicars general, episcopal vicars, or district or regional vicars;

2. or be the parish priests (pastors) of the places where confirmation is conferred, parish priests (pastors) of the places where the candidates belong, or priests who have had a special part in the catechetical preparation of the candidates.[11]

15   Deacons should be ready to assist in the ministry to catechumens. Conferences of bishops that have decided in favor of the permanent diaconate should ensure that the number and distribution of permanent deacons are

---

[8] See ibid., nos. 13–15.

[9] See Vatican Council II, Decree on the Ministry and Life of Priests *Presbyterorum Ordinis,* no. 6.

[10] See *Rite of Confirmation,* Introduction, no. 7.b.

[11] See ibid., no. 8.

adequate for the carrying out of the steps, periods, and formation programs of the catechumenate wherever pastoral needs require.[12]

16   Catechists, who have an important office for the progress of the cate- 48 chumens and for the growth of the community, should, whenever possible, have an active part in the rites. When deputed by the bishop (see no. 12), they may perform the minor exorcisms and blessings contained in the ritual.[13] When they are teaching, catechists should see that their instruction is filled with the spirit of the Gospel, adapted to the liturgical signs and the cycle of the Church's year, suited to the needs of the catechumens, and as far as possible enriched by local traditions.

TIME AND PLACE OF INITIATION

17   As a general rule, parish priests (pastors) should make use of the rite 49 of initiation in such a way that the sacraments themselves are celebrated at the Easter Vigil and the rite of election takes place on the First Sunday of Lent. The rest of the rites are spaced on the basis of the structure and arrangement of the catechumenate as described previously (nos. 6-8). For pastoral needs of a more serious nature, however, it is lawful to arrange the schedule for the entire rite of initiation differently, as will be detailed later (nos. 26–30).

PROPER OR USUAL TIMES

18   The following should be noted about the time of celebrating the rite 50 of acceptance into the order of catechumens (nos. 41–74).

1. It should not be too early, but should be delayed until the candidates, according to their own dispositions and situation, have had sufficient time to conceive an initial faith and to show the first signs of conversion (see no. 42).

2. In places where the number of candidates is smaller than usual, the

---

[2] See Vatican Council II, Dogmatic Constitution on the Church *Lumen gentium*, no. 26; Decree on the Church's Missionary Activity *Ad gentes*, no. 16.
[3] See Vatican Council II, Constitution on the Liturgy *Sacrosanctum Concilium*, art. 79.

rite of acceptance should be delayed until a group is formed that is sufficiently large for catechesis and the liturgical rites.

3. Two dates in the year, or three if necessary, are to be fixed as the usual times for carrying out this rite.

19 The rite of election or enrollment of names (nos. 118–137) should as a rule be celebrated on the First Sunday of Lent. As circumstances suggest or require, it may be anticipated somewhat or even celebrated on a weekday.

20 The scrutinies (nos. 150–156, 164–177) should take place on the Third, Fourth, and Fifth Sundays of Lent, or, if necessary, on the other Sundays of Lent, or even on convenient weekdays. Three scrutinies should be celebrated. The bishop may dispense from one of them for serious reasons or, in extraordinary circumstances, even from two (see nos. 34.3, 331). When, for lack of time, the election is held early, the first scrutiny is also to be held early; but in this case care is to be taken not to prolong the period of purification and enlightenment beyond eight weeks.

21 By ancient usage, the presentations, since they take place after the scrutinies, are part of the same period of purification and enlightenment. They are celebrated during the week. The presentation of the Creed to the catechumens (nos. 157–163) takes place during the week after the first scrutiny; the presentation of the Lord's Prayer (nos. 178–184) during the week after the third scrutiny. For pastoral reasons, however, to enrich the liturgy in the period of the catechumenate, each presentation may be transferred and celebrated during the period of the catechumenate as a kind of "rite of passage" (see nos. 79, 104–105).

22 On Holy Saturday, when the elect refrain from work and spend their time in recollection, the various preparation rites may be celebrated: the recitation or "return" of the Creed by the elect, the ephphetha rite, and the choosing of a Christian name (nos. 185–205).

23 The celebration of the sacraments of Christian initiation (nos. 206–243) should take place at the Easter Vigil itself (see nos. 8, 17). But if there are a great many catechumens, the sacraments are given to the majority that night and reception of the sacraments by the rest may be transferred to days

28

within the Easter octave, whether at the principal church or at a mission station. In this case either the Mass of the day or one of the ritual Masses "Christian Initiation: Baptism" may be used and the readings are chosen from those of the Easter Vigil.

24   In certain cases when there is serious reason, confirmation may be 56 postponed until near the end of the period of postbaptismal catechesis, for example, Pentecost Sunday (see no. 249).

25   On all the Sundays of the Easter season after Easter Sunday, the so-called 57 Masses for neophytes are to be scheduled. The entire community and the newly baptized with their godparents should be encouraged to participate (see nos. 247–248).

OUTSIDE THE USUAL TIMES

26   The entire rite of Christian initiation is normally arranged so that the 58 sacraments will be celebrated during the Easter Vigil. Because of unusual circumstances and pastoral needs, however, the rite of election and the rites belonging to the period of purification and enlightenment may be held outside Lent and the sacraments of initiation may be celebrated at a time other than the Easter Vigil or Easter Sunday.

Even when the usual time has otherwise been observed, it is permissible, but only for serious pastoral needs (for example, if there are a great many people to be baptized), to choose a day other than the Easter Vigil or Easter Sunday, but preferably one during the Easter season, to celebrate the sacraments of initiation; the program of initiation during Lent, however, must be maintained.

When the time is changed in either way, even though the rite of Christian initiation occurs at a different point in the liturgical year, the structure of the entire rite, with its properly spaced intervals, remains the same. But the following adjustments are made.

27   As far as possible, the sacraments of initiation are to be celebrated on 59 a Sunday, using, as occasion suggests, the Sunday Mass or one of the ritual Masses "Christian Initiation: Baptism" (see nos. 23, 208).

28   The rite of acceptance into the order of catechumens is to take place 60
when the time is right (see no. 18).

29   The rite of election is to be celebrated about six weeks before the 6
sacraments of initiation, so that there is sufficient time for the scrutinies and
the presentations. Care should be taken not to schedule the celebration of
the rite of election on a solemnity of the liturgical year.

30   The scrutinies should not be celebrated on solemnities, but on Sundays 6
or even on weekdays, with the usual intervals.

PLACE OF CELEBRATION

31   The rites should be celebrated in the places appropriate to them as 6
indicated in the ritual. Consideration should be given to special needs that
arise in secondary stations of mission territories.

ADAPTATIONS BY THE CONFERENCES OF BISHOPS IN THE USE OF THE ROMAN RITUAL

32   In addition to the adaptations envisioned in *Christian Initiation*, Gen- •
eral Introduction (nos. 30–33), the rite of Christian initiation of adults allows
for other adaptations that will be decided by the conference of bishops.

33   The conference of bishops has discretionary power to make the following decisions:

1. to establish for the precatechumenate, where it seems advisable, some
way of receiving inquirers who are interested in the catechumenate (see
no. 39);

2. to insert into the rite of acceptance into the order of catechumens a
first exorcism and a renunciation of false worship, in regions where pa-
ganism is widespread (see nos. 69–72) [The National Conference of Catholic Bishops has approved leaving to the discretion of the diocesan bishop
this inclusion of a first exorcism and a renunciation of false worship in
the rite of acceptance into the order of catechumens];

3. to decide that in the same rite the tracing of the sign of the cross upon the forehead (nos. 54–55) be replaced by making that sign in front of the forehead, in regions where the act of touching may not seem proper [The National Conference of Catholic Bishops has established as the norm in the dioceses of the United States the tracing of the cross on the forehead. It leaves to the discretion of the diocesan bishop the substitution of making the sign of the cross in front of the forehead for those persons in whose culture the act of touching may not seem proper];

4. to decide that in the same rite candidates receive a new name in regions where it is the practice of non-Christian religions to give a new name to initiates immediately (no. 73) [The National Conference of Catholic Bishops establishes as the norm in the dioceses of the United States that there is to be no giving of a new name. It also approves leaving to the discretion of the diocesan bishop the giving of a new name to persons from those cultures in which it is the practice of non-Christian religions to give a new name];

5. to allow within the same rite, according to local customs, additional rites that symbolize reception into the community (no. 74) [The National Conference of Catholic Bishops has approved the inclusion of an optional presentation of a cross (no. 74) while leaving to the discretion of the diocesan bishop the inclusion of additional rites that symbolize reception into the community];

6. to establish during the period of the catechumenate, in addition to the usual rites (nos. 81–97), "rites of passage": for example, early celebration of the presentations (nos. 157–163, 178–184), the ephphetha rite, the catechumens' recitation of the Creed, or even an anointing of the catechumens (nos. 98–103) [The National Conference of Catholic Bishops approves the use of the anointing with the oil of catechumens during the period of the catechumenate as a kind of "rite of passage" (see no. 33.7). In addition it approves, when appropriate in the circumstances, the early celebration of the presentations (nos. 157–163, 178–184), the ephphetha rite (nos. 197–199), and the catechumens' recitation of the Creed (nos. 193–196)];

7. to decide on the omission of the anointing with the oil of catechumens or its transferral to the preparation rites for Holy Saturday or its use during the period of the catechumenate as a kind of "rite of passage" (nos. 98–

103) [The National Conference of Catholic Bishops approves the omission of the anointing with the oil of catechumens both in the celebration of baptism and in the optional preparation rites for Holy Saturday. Thus, anointing with the oil of catechumens is reserved for use in the period of the catechumenate and in the period of purification and enlightenment and is not to be included in the preparation rites on Holy Saturday or in the celebration of initiation at the Easter Vigil or at another time];

8. to make more specific and detailed the formularies of renunciation for the rite of acceptance into the order of catechumens (nos. 70–72) and for the celebration of baptism (no. 224) [The National Conference of Catholic Bishops has established as the norm in the dioceses of the United States that the formularies of renunciation should not be adapted. But for those cases where certain catechumens may be from cultures in which false worship is widespread it has approved leaving to the discretion of the diocesan bishop this matter of making more specific and detailed the formularies of renunciation in the rite of acceptance into the order of catechumens and in the celebration of baptism].

ADAPTATIONS BY THE BISHOP

34 It pertains to the bishop for his own diocese:

1. to set up the formation program of the catechumenate and to lay down norms according to local needs (see no. 12);

2. to decide whether and when, as circumstances warrant, the entire rite of Christian initiation may be celebrated outside the usual times (see no. 26);

3. to dispense, on the basis of some serious obstacle, from one scrutiny or, in extraordinary circumstances, even from two (see no. 331);

4. to permit the simple rite to be used in whole or in part (see no. 331);

5. to depute catechists, truly worthy and properly prepared, to give the exorcisms and blessings (see nos. 12, 16);

6. to preside at the rite of election and to ratify, personally or through a delegate, the admission of the elect (see no. 12);

7. in keeping with the provisions of law,[14] to stipulate the requisite age for sponsors (see *Christian Initiation,* General Introduction, no. 10.2).

ADAPTATIONS BY THE MINISTER

35 Celebrants should make full and intelligent use of the freedom given to them either in *Christian Initiation,* General Introduction (no. 34) or in the rubrics of the rite itself. In many places the manner of acting or praying is intentionally left undetermined or two alternatives are offered, so that ministers, according to their prudent pastoral judgment, may accommodate the rite to the circumstances of the candidates and others who are present. In all the rites the greatest freedom is left in the invitations and instructions, and the intercessions may always be shortened, changed, or even expanded with new intentions, in order to fit the circumstances or special situation of the candidates (for example, a sad or joyful event occurring in a family) or of the others present (for example, sorrow or joy common to a parish or civic community).

The minister will also adapt the texts by changing the gender and number as required.

---

[14] See *Codex Iuris Canonici,* can. 874, §1, 2°.

PART I

CHRISTIAN INITIATION
OF ADULTS

OUTLINE FOR CHRISTIAN INITIATION OF ADULTS

PERIOD OF EVANGELIZATION AND PRECATECHUMENATE
This is a time, of no fixed duration or structure, for inquiry and introduction to Gospel values, an opportunity for the beginnings of faith.

FIRST STEP: ACCEPTANCE INTO THE ORDER OF CATECHUMENS
This is the liturgical rite, usually celebrated on some annual date or dates, marking the beginning of the catechumenate proper, as the candidates express and the Church accepts their intention to respond to God's call to follow the way of Christ.

PERIOD OF THE CATECHUMENATE
This is the time, in duration corresponding to the progress of the individual, for the nurturing and growth of the catechumens' faith and conversion to God; celebrations of the word and prayers of exorcism and blessing are meant to assist the process.

SECOND STEP: ELECTION OR ENROLLMENT OF NAMES
This is the liturgical rite, usually celebrated on the First Sunday of Lent, by which the Church formally ratifies the catechumens' readiness for the sacraments of initiation and the catechumens, now the elect, express the will to receive these sacraments.

PERIOD OF PURIFICATION AND ENLIGHTENMENT
This is the time immediately preceding the elects' initiation, usually the Lenten season preceding the celebration of this initiation at the Easter Vigil; it is a time of reflection, intensely centered on conversion, marked by celebration of the scrutinies and presentations and of the preparation rites on Holy Saturday.

THIRD STEP: CELEBRATION OF THE SACRAMENTS OF INITIATION

This is the liturgical rite, usually integrated into the Easter Vigil, by which the elect are initiated through baptism, confirmation, and the eucharist.

PERIOD OF POSTBAPTISMAL CATECHESIS OR MYSTAGOGY

This is the time, usually the Easter season, following the celebration of initiation, during which the newly initiated experience being fully a part of the Christian community by means of pertinent catechesis and particularly by participation with all the faithful in the Sunday eucharistic celebration.

PERIOD OF EVANGELIZATION AND PRECATECHUMENATE

36 Although the rite of initiation begins with admission to the catechu- 9
menate, the preceding period or precatechumenate is of great importance and as a rule should not be omitted. It is a time of evangelization: faithfully and constantly the living God is proclaimed and Jesus Christ whom he has sent for the salvation of all. Thus those who are not yet Christians, their hearts opened by the Holy Spirit, may believe and be freely converted to the Lord and commit themselves sincerely to him. For he who is the way, the truth, and the life fulfills all their spiritual expectations, indeed infinitely surpasses them.[1]

37 From evangelization, completed with the help of God, come the faith
and initial conversion that cause a person to feel called away from sin and drawn into the mystery of God's love. The whole period of the precatechumenate is set aside for this evangelization, so that the genuine will to follow Christ and seek baptism may mature.

38 During this period, priests and deacons, catechists and other laypersons are to give the candidates a suitable explanation of the Gospel (see no. 42). The candidates are to receive help and attention so that with a purified and

---

[1] See Vatican Council II, Decree on the Church's Missionary Activity *Ad gentes*, no. 13.

clearer intention they may cooperate with God's grace. Opportunities should be provided for them to meet families and other groups of Christians.

39   It belongs to the conference of bishops to provide for the evangelization 12 proper to this period. The conference may also provide, if circumstances suggest and in keeping with local custom, a preliminary manner of receiving those interested in the precatechumenate, that is, those inquirers who, even though they do not fully believe, show some leaning toward the Christian faith (and who may be called "sympathizers").

1. Such a reception, if it takes place, will be carried out without any ritual celebration; it is the expression not yet of faith, but of a right intention.

2. The reception will be adapted to local conditions and to the pastoral situation. Some candidates may need to see evidence of the spirit of Christians that they are striving to understand and experience. For others, however, whose catechumenate will be delayed for one reason or another, some initial act of the candidates or the community that expresses their reception may be appropriate.

3. The reception will be held at a meeting or gathering of the local community, on an occasion that will permit friendly conversation. An inquirer or "sympathizer" is introduced by a friend and then welcomed and received by the priest or some other representative member of the community.

40   During the precatechumenate period, parish priests (pastors) should 13 help those taking part in it with prayers suited to them, for example, by 111 celebrating for their spiritual well-being the prayers of exorcism and the 120 blessings given in the ritual (nos. 94, 97).

FIRST STEP: ACCEPTANCE INTO THE ORDER OF CATECHUMENS

41   The rite that is called the rite of acceptance into the order of catechu- 14 mens is of the utmost importance. Assembling publicly for the first time, the 15 candidates who have completed the period of the precatechumenate declare 68 their intention to the Church and the Church in turn, carrying out its apostolic

mission, accepts them as persons who intend to become its members. God showers his grace on the candidates, since the celebration manifests their desire publicly and marks their reception and first consecration by the Church.

42   The prerequisite for making this first step is that the beginnings of the spiritual life and the fundamentals of Christian teaching have taken root in the candidates.[1] Thus there must be evidence of the first faith that was conceived during the period of evangelization and precatechumenate and of an initial conversion and intention to change their lives and to enter into a relationship with God in Christ. Consequently, there must also be evidence of the first stirrings of repentance, a start to the practice of calling upon God in prayer, a sense of the Church, and some experience of the company and spirit of Christians through contact with a priest or with members of the community. The candidates should also be instructed about the celebration of the liturgical rite of acceptance.

43   Before the rite is celebrated, therefore, sufficient and necessary time, as required in each case, should be set aside to evaluate and, if necessary, to purify the candidates' motives and dispositions. With the help of the sponsors (see no. 10), catechists, and deacons, parish priests (pastors) have the responsibility for judging the outward indications of such dispositions.[2] Because of the effect of baptism once validly received (see *Christian Initiation*, General Introduction, no. 4), it is the duty of parish priests (pastors) to see to it that no baptized person seeks for any reason whatever to be baptized a second time.

44   The rite will take place on specified days during the year (see no. 18) that are suited to local conditions. The rite consists in the reception of the candidates, the celebration of the word of God, and the dismissal of the candidates; celebration of the eucharist may follow.
   By decision of the conference of bishops, the following may be incorporated into this rite: a first exorcism and renunciation of false worship (nos. 70–72), the giving of a new name (no. 73), and additional rites signifying reception into the community (no. 74). [See no. 33 for the decisions made by the National Conference of Catholic Bishops regarding these matters.]

---

[1] See Vatican Council II, Decree on the Church's Missionary Activity *Ad gentes*, no. 14.
[2] See ibid., no. 13.

45   It is desirable that the entire Christian community or some part of it, 70
consisting of friends and acquaintances, catechists and priests, take an active 71
part in the celebration. The presiding celebrant is a priest or a deacon. The
sponsors should also attend in order to present to the Church the candidates
they have brought.

46   After the celebration of the rite of acceptance, the names of the cate- 17
chumens are to be duly inscribed in the register of catechumens, along with
the names of the sponsors and the minister and the date and place of the
celebration.

47   From this time on the Church embraces the catechumens as its own 18
with a mother's love and concern. Joined to the Church, the catechumens
are now part of the household of Christ,[3] since the Church nourishes them
with the word of God and sustains them by means of liturgical celebrations.
The catechumens should be eager, then, to take part in celebrations of the
word of God and to receive blessings and other sacramentals. When two
catechumens marry or when a catechumen marries an unbaptized person,
the appropriate rite is to be used.[4] One who dies during the catechumenate
receives a Christian burial.

---

[3] See Vatican Council II, Dogmatic Constitution on the Church *Lumen gentium*, no. 14;
Decree on the Church's Missionary Activity *Ad gentes*, no. 14.

[4] See *Rite of Marriage*, nos. 55–66.

OUTLINE OF THE RITE

RECEIVING THE CANDIDATES

Greeting
Opening Dialogue
Candidates' First Acceptance of the Gospel
Affirmation by the Sponsors and the Assembly
Signing of the Candidates with the Cross
   Signing of the Forehead
   [Signing of the Other Senses]
   Concluding Prayer
Invitation to the Celebration of the Word of God

LITURGY OF THE WORD

Instruction
Readings
Homily
[Presentation of a Bible]
Intercessions for the Catechumens
Prayer over the Catechumens
Dismissal of the Catechumens

LITURGY OF THE EUCHARIST

PERIOD OF THE CATECHUMENATE

75   The catechumenate is an extended period during which the candidates are given suitable pastoral formation and guidance, aimed at training them in the Christian life.[1] In this way, the dispositions manifested at their acceptance into the catechumenate are brought to maturity. This is achieved in four ways.

1. A suitable catechesis is provided by priests or deacons, or by catechists and others of the faithful, planned to be gradual and complete in its coverage, accommodated to the liturgical year, and solidly supported by celebrations of the word. This catechesis leads the catechumens not only to an appropriate acquaintance with dogmas and precepts but also to a profound sense of the mystery of salvation in which they desire to participate.

2. As they become familiar with the Christian way of life and are helped by the example and support of sponsors, godparents, and the entire Christian community, the catechumens learn to turn more readily to God in prayer, to bear witness to the faith, in all things to keep their hopes set on Christ, to follow supernatural inspiration in their deeds, and to practice love of neighbor, even at the cost of self-renunciation. Thus formed, "the newly converted set out on a spiritual journey. Already sharing through faith in the mystery of Christ's death and resurrection, they pass from the old to a new nature made perfect in Christ. Since this transition brings with it a progressive change of outlook and conduct, it should become manifest by means of its social consequences and it should develop gradually during the period of the catechumenate. Since the Lord in whom they believe is a sign of contradiction, the newly converted often experience divisions and separations, but they also taste the joy that God gives without measure."[2]

3. The Church, like a mother, helps the catechumens on their journey by means of suitable liturgical rites, which purify the catechumens little by little and strengthen them with God's blessing. Celebrations of the word of God are arranged for their benefit, and at Mass they may also take part with the faithful in the liturgy of the word, thus better preparing themselves

---

[1] See Vatican Council II, Decree on the Church's Missionary Activity *Ad gentes,* no. 14.
[2] Ibid., no. 13.

for their eventual participation in the liturgy of the eucharist. Ordinarily, however, when they are present in the assembly of the faithful they should be kindly dismissed before the liturgy of the eucharist begins (unless their dismissal would present practical or pastoral problems). For they must await their baptism, which will join them to God's priestly people and empower them to participate in Christ's new worship (see no. 67 for formularies of dismissal).

4. Since the Church's life is apostolic, catechumens should also learn how to work actively with others to spread the Gospel and build up the Church by the witness of their lives and by professing their faith.[3]

76   The duration of the catechumenate will depend on the grace of God and on various circumstances, such as the program of instruction for the catechumenate, the number of catechists, deacons, and priests, the cooperation of the individual catechumens, the means necessary for them to come to the site of the catechumenate and spend time there, the help of the local community. Nothing, therefore, can be settled a priori.

The time spent in the catechumenate should be long enough—several years if necessary—for the conversion and faith of the catechumens to become strong. By their formation in the entire Christian life and a sufficiently prolonged probation the catechumens are properly initiated into the mysteries of salvation and the practice of an evangelical way of life. By means of sacred rites celebrated at successive times they are led into the life of faith, worship, and charity belonging to the people of God.

77   It is the responsibility of the bishop to fix the duration and to direct the program of the catechumenate. The conference of bishops, after considering the conditions of its people and region,[4] may also wish to provide specific guidelines. At the discretion of the bishop, on the basis of the spiritual preparation of the candidate, the period of the catechumenate may in particular cases be shortened (see nos. 331–335); in altogether extraordinary cases the catechumenate may be completed all at once (see nos. 332, 336–369).

78   The instruction that the catechumens receive during this period should

---

[3] See Vatican Council II, Decree on the Church's Missionary Activity *Ad gentes,* no. 14.
[4] See Vatican Council II, Constitution on the Liturgy *Sacrosanctum Concilium,* art. 64.

be of a kind that while presenting Catholic teaching in its entirety also enlightens faith, directs the heart toward God, fosters participation in the liturgy, inspires apostolic activity, and nurtures a life completely in accord with the spirit of Christ.

79 Among the rites belonging to the period of the catechumenate, then, 103 celebrations of the word of God (nos. 81–89) are foremost. The minor exorcisms (nos. 90–94) and the blessings of the catechumens (nos. 95–97) are ordinarily celebrated in conjunction with a celebration of the word. In addition, other rites may be celebrated to mark the passage of the catechumens from one level of catechesis to another: for example, an anointing of the catechumens may be celebrated (nos. 98–103) and the presentations of the Creed and the Lord's Prayer may be anticipated (see nos. 104–105).

80 During the period of the catechumenate, the catechumens should give 104 thought to choosing the godparents who will present them to the Church 105 on the day of their election (see no. 11; also *Christian Initiation*, General Introduction, nos. 8–10).

Provision should also be made for the entire community involved in the formation of the catechumens—priests, deacons, catechists, sponsors, godparents, friends and neighbors—to participate in some of the celebrations belonging to the catechumenate, including any of the optional "rites of passage" (nos. 98–105).

RITES BELONGING TO THE PERIOD OF THE CATECHUMENATE

CELEBRATIONS OF THE WORD OF GOD

81 During the period of the catechumenate there should be celebrations 100 of the word of God that accord with the liturgical season and that contribute to the instruction of the catechumens and the needs of the community. These celebrations of the word are: first, celebrations held specially for the catechumens; second, participation in the liturgy of the word at the Sunday Mass; third, celebrations held in connection with catechetical instruction.

82 The special celebrations of the word of God arranged for the benefit of the catechumens have as their main purpose:

1. to implant in their hearts the teachings they are receiving: for example, the morality characteristic of the New Testament, the forgiving of injuries and insults, a sense of sin and repentance, the duties Christians must carry out in the world;

2. to give them instruction and experience in the different aspects and ways of prayer;

3. to explain to them the signs, celebrations, and seasons of the liturgy;

4. to prepare them gradually to enter the worship assembly of the entire community.

83 From the very beginning of the period of the catechumenate the ca-techumens should be taught to keep holy the Lord's Day.

1. Care should be taken that some of the special celebrations of the word just mentioned (no. 82) are held on Sunday, so that the catechumens will become accustomed to taking an active and practiced part in these celebrations.

2. Gradually the catechumens should be admitted to the first part of the celebration of the Sunday Mass. After the liturgy of the word they should, if possible, be dismissed, but an intention for them is included in the general intercessions (see no. 67 for formularies of dismissal).

84 Celebrations of the word may also be held in connection with cate-chetical or instructional meetings of the catechumens, so that these will occur in a context of prayer.

MODEL FOR A CELEBRATION OF THE WORD OF GOD

85 For the celebrations of the word of God that are held specially for the benefit of the catechumens (see no. 82), the following structure (nos. 86–89) may be used as a model.

86 SONG: An appropriate song may be sung to open the celebration.

87 READINGS AND RESPONSORIAL PSALMS: One or more readings from Scripture, chosen for their relevance to the formation of the catechumens, are proclaimed by a baptized member of the community. A sung responsorial psalm should ordinarily follow each reading.

88 HOMILY: A brief homily that explains and applies the readings should be given.

89 CONCLUDING RITES: The celebration of the word may conclude with a USA minor exorcism (no. 94) or with a blessing of the catechumens (no. 97). When the minor exorcism is used, it may be followed by one of the blessings (no. 97) or, on occasion, by the rite of anointing (nos. 102–103).*

MINOR EXORCISMS

90 The first or minor exorcisms have been composed in the form of pe- 101 titions directly addressed to God. They draw the attention of the catechumens to the real nature of Christian life, the struggle between flesh and spirit, the importance of self-denial for reaching the blessedness of God's kingdom, and the unending need for God's help.

91 The presiding celebrant for the minor exorcisms is a priest, a deacon, 109 or a qualified catechist appointed by the bishop for this ministry (see no. 16).

92 The minor exorcisms take place within a celebration of the word of 110 God held in a church, a chapel, or in a center for the catechumenate. A minor exorcism may also be held at the beginning or end of a meeting for

---

* Celebrations of the word that are held in connection with instructional sessions may include, along with an appropriate reading, a minor exorcism (no. 94) or a blessing of the catechumens (no. 97). When the minor exorcism is used, it may be followed by one of the blessings (no. 97) or, on occasion, by the rite of anointing (nos. 102–103).

The meetings of the catechumens after the liturgy of the word of the Sunday Mass may also include a minor exorcism (no. 94) or a blessing (no. 97). Likewise, when the minor exorcism is used, it may be followed by one of the blessings (no. 97) or, on occasion, by the rite of anointing (nos. 102–103).

catechesis. When there is some special need, one of these prayers of exorcism may be said privately for individual catechumens.

93   The formularies for the minor exorcisms may be used on several oc- 1 casions, as different situations may suggest.

BLESSINGS OF THE CATECHUMENS

95   The blessings of the catechumens are a sign of God's love and of the 1 Church's tender care. They are bestowed on the catechumens so that, even though they do not as yet have the grace of the sacraments, they may still receive from the Church courage, joy, and peace as they proceed along the difficult journey they have begun.

96   The blessings may be given by a priest, a deacon, or a qualified catechist appointed by the bishop (see no. 16). The blessings are usually given at the end of a celebration of the word; they may also be given at the end of a meeting for catechesis. When there is some special need, the blessings may be given privately to individual catechumens.

ANOINTING OF THE CATECHUMENS

98   During the period of the catechumenate, a rite of anointing the cate-chumens, through use of the oil of catechumens, may be celebrated wherever this seems beneficial or desirable. The presiding celebrant for such a first anointing of the catechumens is a priest or a deacon.

99   Care is to be taken that the catechumens understand the significance of the anointing with oil. The anointing with oil symbolizes their need for God's help and strength so that, undeterred by the bonds of the past and overcoming the opposition of the devil, they will forthrightly take the step of professing their faith and will hold fast to it unfalteringly throughout their lives.

100   The anointing ordinarily takes place after the homily in a celebration of the word of God (see no. 89), and is conferred on each of the catechumens;

48

this rite of anointing may be celebrated several times during the course of the catechumenate. Further, for particular reasons, a priest or a deacon may confer the anointing privately on individual catechumens.

101   The oil used for this rite is to be the oil blessed by the bishop at the 129 chrism Mass, but for pastoral reasons a priest celebrant may bless oil for the rite immediately before the anointing.

PRESENTATIONS [OPTIONAL]

104   The presentations normally take place during Lent, the period of pu- 125 rification and enlightenment, after the first and third scrutinies. But for pastoral advantage and because the period of purification and enlightenment is rather short, the presentations may be held during the period of the cate-chumenate, rather than at the regular times. But the presentations are not to take place until a point during the catechumenate when the catechumens are judged ready for these celebrations.

105   Both the presentation of the Creed and the presentation of the Lord's 126 Prayer may be anticipated; each may be concluded with the ephphetha rite.[1] When the presentations are anticipated, care is to be taken to substitute the term "catechumens" for the term "elect" in all formularies.

SENDING OF THE CATECHUMENS USA
FOR ELECTION [OPTIONAL]

106   At the conclusion of the period of the catechumenate, a rite of sending the catechumens to their election by the bishop may be celebrated in parishes wherever this seems beneficial or desirable. When election will take place in the parish, this rite is not used.

107   As the focal point of the Church's concern for the catechumens, ad-mission to election belongs to the bishop who is usually its presiding cel-

----

[1] But if the rite of recitation of the Creed (nos. 193–196) is also anticipated as one of the "rites of passage" (see no. 33.6), the ephphetha rite is used only to begin this rite of recitation and not with the presentations.

ebrant. It is within the parish community, however, that the preliminary judgment is made concerning the catechumens' state of formation and progress.

This rite offers that local community the opportunity to express its approval of the catechumens and to send them forth to the celebration of election assured of the parish's care and support.

108   The rite is celebrated in the parish church at a suitable time prior to the rite of election.

109   The rite takes place after the homily in a celebration of the word of God (see no. 89) or at Mass.

110   When the Rite of Sending Catechumens for Election is combined with the rite of sending for recognition by the bishop the (already baptized) adult candidates for the sacraments of confirmation and eucharist (or: for reception into the full communion of the Catholic Church), the alternate rite found on page 289 (Appendix I, 2) is used.

SECOND STEP: ELECTION OR ENROLLMENT OF NAMES

118   The second step in Christian initiation is the liturgical rite called both election and the enrollment of names, which closes the period of the catechumenate proper, that is, the lengthy period of formation of the catechumens' minds and hearts. The celebration of the rite of election, which usually coincides with the opening of Lent, also marks the beginning of the period of final, more intense preparation for the sacraments of initiation, during which the elect will be encouraged to follow Christ with greater generosity.

119   At this second step, on the basis of the testimony of godparents and catechists and of the catechumens' reaffirmation of their intention, the Church judges their state of readiness and decides on their advancement toward the sacraments of initiation. Thus the Church makes its "election," that is, the choice and admission of those catechumens who have the dispositions that

make them fit to take part, at the next major celebration, in the sacraments of initiation.

This step is called election because the acceptance made by the Church is founded on the election by God, in whose name the Church acts. The step is also called the enrollment of names because as a pledge of fidelity the candidates inscribe their names in the book that lists those who have been chosen for initiation.

120   Before the rite of election is celebrated, the catechumens are expected 23 to have undergone a conversion in mind and in action and to have developed a sufficient acquaintance with Christian teaching as well as a spirit of faith and charity. With deliberate will and an enlightened faith they must have the intention to receive the sacraments of the Church, a resolve they will express publicly in the actual celebration of the rite.

121   The election, marked with a rite of such solemnity, is the focal point 135 of the Church's concern for the catechumens. Admission to election therefore belongs to the bishop, and the presiding celebrant for the rite of election is the bishop himself or a priest or a deacon who acts as the bishop's delegate (see no. 12).

Before the rite of election the bishop, priests, deacons, catechists, godparents, and the entire community, in accord with their respective responsibilities and in their own way, should, after considering the matter carefully, arrive at a judgment about the catechumens' state of formation and progress. After the election, they should surround the elect with prayer, so that the entire Church will accompany and lead them to encounter Christ.

122   Within the rite of election the bishop celebrant or his delegate declares 23 in the presence of the community the Church's approval of the candidates. [137] Therefore to exclude any semblance of mere formality from the rite, there should be a deliberation prior to its celebration to decide on the catechumens' suitableness. This deliberation is carried out by the priests, deacons, and catechists involved in the formation of the catechumens, and by the godparents and representatives of the local community. If circumstances suggest, the group of catechumens may also take part. The deliberation may take various forms, depending on local conditions and pastoral needs. During the celebration of election, the assembly is informed of the decision approving the catechumens.

123   Before the rite of election godparents are chosen by the catechumens the choice should be made with the consent of the priest, and the persons chosen should, as far as possible, be approved for their role by the local community (see no. 11). In the rite of election the godparents exercise their ministry publicly for the first time. They are called by name at the beginning of the rite to come forward with the catechumens (no. 130); they give testimony on behalf of the catechumens before the community (no. 131) they may also write their names along with the catechumens in the book of the elect (no. 132).

124   From the day of their election and admission, the catechumens are called "the elect." They are also described as *competentes* ("co-petitioners"), because they are joined together in asking for and aspiring to receive the three sacraments of Christ and the gift of the Holy Spirit. They are also called *illuminandi* ("those who will be enlightened"), because baptism itself has been called *illuminatio* ("enlightenment") and it fills the newly baptized with the light of faith. In our own times, other names may be applied to the elect that, depending on regions and cultures, are better suited to the people's understanding and the idiom of the language.

125   The bishop celebrant or his delegate, however much or little he was involved in the deliberation prior to the rite, has the responsibility of showing in the homily or elsewhere during the celebration the religious and ecclesial significance of the election. The celebrant also declares before all present the Church's decision and, if appropriate in the circumstances, asks the community to express its approval of the candidates. He also asks the catechumens to give a personal expression of their intention and, in the name of the Church, he carries out the act of admitting them as elect. The celebrant should open to all the divine mystery expressed in the call of the Church and in the liturgical celebration of this mystery. He should remind the faithful to give good example to the elect and along with the elect to prepare themselves for the Easter solemnities.

126   The sacraments of initiation are celebrated during the Easter solemnities, and preparation for these sacraments is part of the distinctive character of Lent. Accordingly, the rite of election should normally take place on the First Sunday of Lent and the period of final preparation of the elect should coincide with the Lenten season. The plan arranged for the Lenten season

will benefit the elect by reason of both its liturgical structure and the participation of the community. For urgent pastoral reasons, especially in secondary mission stations, it is permitted to celebrate the rite of election during the week preceding or following the First Sunday of Lent.

When, because of unusual circumstances and pastoral needs, the rite of election is celebrated outside Lent, it is to be celebrated about six weeks before the sacraments of initiation, in order to allow sufficient time for the scrutinies and presentations. The rite is not to be celebrated on a solemnity of the liturgical year (see no. 29).

127   The rite should take place in the cathedral church, in a parish church or, if necessary, in some other suitable and fitting place. 140 USA

128   The rite is celebrated within Mass, after the homily, and should be celebrated within the Mass of the First Sunday of Lent. If, for pastoral reasons, the rite is celebrated on a different day, the texts and the readings of the ritual Mass "Christian Initiation: Election or Enrollment of Names" may always be used. When the Mass of the day is celebrated and its readings are not suitable, the readings are those given for the First Sunday of Lent or others may be chosen from elsewhere in the Lectionary. 140 141

When celebrated outside Mass, the rite takes place after the readings and the homily and is concluded with the dismissal of both the elect and the faithful.

[An optional parish rite to send catechumens for election by the bishop precedes the rite of election and is found at no. 106.]

OUTLINE OF THE RITE

LITURGY OF THE WORD

Homily
Presentation of the Catechumens
Affirmation by the Godparents [and the Assembly]
Invitation and Enrollment of Names
Act of Admission or Election
Intercessions for the Elect
Prayer over the Elect
Dismissal of the Elect

LITURGY OF THE EUCHARIST

PERIOD OF PURIFICATION AND ENLIGHTENMENT

138   The period of purification and enlightenment, which the rite of election 21
begins, customarily coincides with Lent. In the liturgy and liturgical cate- 152
chesis of Lent the reminder of baptism already received or the preparation
for its reception, as well as the theme of repentance, renew the entire
community along with those being prepared to celebrate the paschal mystery,
in which each of the elect will share through the sacraments of initiation.[1]
For both the elect and the local community, therefore, the Lenten season is
a time for spiritual recollection in preparation for the celebration of the
paschal mystery.

139   This is a period of more intense spiritual preparation, consisting more 22
in interior reflection than in catechetical instruction, and is intended to purify 153
the minds and hearts of the elect as they search their own consciences and
do penance. This period is intended as well to enlighten the minds and hearts
of the elect with a deeper knowledge of Christ the Savior. The celebration
of certain rites, particularly the scrutinies (see nos. 141–146) and the presentations (see nos. 147–149), brings about this process of purification and
enlightenment and extends it over the course of the entire Lenten season.

140   Holy Saturday is the day of proximate preparation for the celebration 26
of the sacraments of initiation and on that day the rites of preparation (see
nos. 185–192) may be celebrated.

RITES BELONGING TO THE PERIOD OF PURIFICATION AND ENLIGHTENMENT

SCRUTINIES

41   The scrutinies, which are solemnly celebrated on Sundays and are 25
reinforced by an exorcism, are rites for self-searching and repentance and 154

See Vatican Council II, Decree on the Church's Missionary Activity *Ad gentes,* no. 14.

have above all a spiritual purpose. The scrutinies are meant to uncover, then heal all that is weak, defective, or sinful in the hearts of the elect; to bring out, then strengthen all that is upright, strong, and good. For the scrutinies are celebrated in order to deliver the elect from the power of sin and Satan, to protect them against temptation, and to give them strength in Christ, who is the way, the truth, and the life. These rites, therefore, should complete the conversion of the elect and deepen their resolve to hold fast to Christ and to carry out their decision to love God above all.

142   Because they are asking for the three sacraments of initiation, the elect must have the intention of achieving an intimate knowledge of Christ and his Church, and they are expected particularly to progress in genuine self-knowledge through serious examination of their lives and true repentance.

143   In order to inspire in the elect a desire for purification and redemption by Christ, three scrutinies are celebrated. By this means, first of all, the elect are instructed gradually about the mystery of sin, from which the whole world and every person longs to be delivered and thus saved from its present and future consequences. Second, their spirit is filled with Christ the Redeemer, who is the living water (gospel of the Samaritan woman in the first scrutiny), the light of the world (gospel of the man born blind in the second scrutiny), the resurrection and the life (gospel of Lazarus in the third scrutiny). From the first to the final scrutiny the elect should progress in their perception of sin and their desire for salvation.

144   In the rite of exorcism (nos. 154, 168, 175), which is celebrated by a priest or a deacon, the elect, who have already learned from the Church as their mother the mystery of deliverance from sin by Christ, are freed from the effects of sin and from the influence of the devil. They receive new strength in the midst of their spiritual journey and they open their hearts to receive the gifts of the Savior.

145   The priest or deacon who is the presiding celebrant should carry out the celebration in such a way that the faithful in the assembly will also derive benefit from the liturgy of the scrutinies and join in the intercessions for the elect.

146   The scrutinies should take place within the ritual Masses "Christian

Initiation: The Scrutinies," which are celebrated on the Third, Fourth, and Fifth Sundays of Lent; the readings with their chants are those given for these Sundays in the Lectionary for Mass, Year A. When, for pastoral reasons, these ritual Masses cannot be celebrated on their proper Sundays, they are celebrated on other Sundays of Lent or even convenient days during the week.

When, because of unusual circumstances and pastoral needs, the period of purification and enlightenment takes place outside Lent, the scrutinies are celebrated on Sundays or even on weekdays, with the usual intervals between celebrations. They are not celebrated on solemnities of the liturgical year (see no. 30).

In every case the ritual Masses "Christian Initiation: The Scrutinies" are celebrated and in this sequence: for the first scrutiny the Mass with the gospel of the Samaritan woman; for the second, the Mass with the gospel of the man born blind; for the third, the Mass with the gospel of Lazarus.

PRESENTATIONS

147 The presentations take place after the celebration of the scrutinies, 25 unless, for pastoral reasons, they have been anticipated during the period of [181] the catechumenate (see nos. 79, 104–105). Thus, with the catechumenal formation of the elect completed, the Church lovingly entrusts to them the Creed and the Lord's Prayer, the ancient texts that have always been regarded as expressing the heart of the Church's faith and prayer. These texts are presented in order to enlighten the elect. The Creed, as it recalls the wonderful deeds of God for the salvation of the human race, suffuses the vision of the elect with the sure light of faith. The Lord's Prayer fills them with a deeper realization of the new spirit of adoption by which they will call God their Father, especially in the midst of the eucharistic assembly.

148 The first presentation to the elect is the presentation of the Creed, 183 during the week following the first scrutiny. The elect are to commit the [184] Creed to memory and they will recite it publicly (nos. 193–196) prior to professing their faith in accordance with that Creed on the day of their baptism.

149 The second presentation to the elect is the presentation of the Lord's 188 Prayer, during the week following the third scrutiny (but, if necessary, this [189]

presentation may be deferred for inclusion in the preparation rites of Holy Saturday; see no. 185). From antiquity the Lord's Prayer has been the prayer proper to those who in baptism have received the spirit of adoption. When the elect have been baptized and take part in their first celebration of the eucharist, they will join the rest of the faithful in saying the Lord's Prayer.

OUTLINE OF THE RITE: SCRUTINIES

LITURGY OF THE WORD

Readings
Homily
Invitation to Silent Prayer
Intercessions for the Elect
Exorcism
Dismissal of the Elect

LITURGY OF THE EUCHARIST

OUTLINE OF THE RITE: PRESENTATION OF THE CREED

LITURGY OF THE WORD

Readings
Homily
Presentation of the Creed
Prayer over the Elect
Dismissal of the Elect

LITURGY OF THE EUCHARIST

OUTLINE OF THE RITE: PRESENTATION OF THE LORD'S PRAYER

LITURGY OF THE WORD

Readings
Gospel Reading (Presentation of the Lord's Prayer)
Homily
Prayer over the Elect
Dismissal of the Elect

LITURGY OF THE EUCHARIST

PREPARATION RITES
ON HOLY SATURDAY

185   In proximate preparation for the celebration of the sacraments of initiation: 26
193

1. The elect are to be advised that on Holy Saturday they should refrain from their usual activities, spend their time in prayer and reflection, and, as far as they can, observe a fast.

2. When it is possible to bring the elect together on Holy Saturday for reflection and prayer, some or all of the following rites may be celebrated as an immediate preparation for the sacraments: the presentation of the Lord's Prayer, if it has been deferred (see nos. 149, 178–180), the "return" or recitation of the Creed (nos. 193–196), the ephphetha rite (nos. 197–199), and the choosing of a baptismal name (nos. 200–202).

186   The choice and arrangement of these rites should be guided by what best suits the particular circumstances of the elect, but the following should be observed with regard to their celebration: 195
197

1. In cases where celebration of the presentation of the Creed was not possible, the recitation of the Creed is not celebrated.

2. When both the recitation of the Creed and the ephphetha rite are celebrated, the ephphetha rite immediately precedes the "Prayer before the Recitation" (no. 194).

MODEL FOR A CELEBRATION OF THE PREPARATION RITES

187   SONG: When the elect have gathered, the celebration begins with a suitable song.

188   GREETING: After the singing, the celebrant greets the elect and any of the faithful who are present, using one of the greetings for Mass or other suitable words.

189   READING OF THE WORD OF GOD: Where indicated in the particular rites, the reading of the word of God follows; the readings may be chosen from those suggested for each rite. If more than one reading is used, a suitable psalm or hymn may be sung between the readings.

190   HOMILY: Where indicated in the particular rites, a brief homily or an explanation of the text follows the reading of the word of God.

191   CELEBRATION OF THE RITES CHOSEN: See nos. 193–202.

192   CONCLUDING RITES: The celebration may be concluded with the prayer of blessing and dismissal given in nos. 204–205.

THIRD STEP: CELEBRATION OF THE SACRAMENTS OF INITIATION

206   The third step in the Christian initiation of adults is the celebration of the sacraments of baptism, confirmation, and eucharist. Through this final step the elect, receiving pardon for their sins, are admitted into the people of God. They are graced with adoption as children of God and are led by the Holy Spirit into the promised fullness of time begun in Christ[1] and, as they share in the eucharistic sacrifice and meal, even to a foretaste of the kingdom of God.

207   The usual time for the celebration of the sacraments of initiation is the Easter Vigil (see no. 23), at which preferably the bishop himself presides as celebrant, at least for the initiation of those who are fourteen years old or older (see no. 12). As indicated in the Roman Missal, "Easter Vigil" (no. 44), the conferral of the sacraments follows the blessing of the water.

208   When the celebration takes place outside the usual time (see nos. 26–27), care should be taken to ensure that it has a markedly paschal character (see *Christian Initiation*, General Introduction, no. 6). Thus the texts for one of the ritual Masses "Christian Initiation: Baptism" given in the Roman

[1] See Vatican Council II, Dogmatic Constitution on the Church *Lumen gentium*, no. 48; also Ephesians 1:10.

Missal are used, and the readings are chosen from those given in the Lectionary for Mass, "Celebration of the Sacraments of Initiation apart from the Easter Vigil."

CELEBRATION OF BAPTISM

209   The celebration of baptism has as its center and high point the baptismal washing and the invocation of the Holy Trinity. Beforehand there are rites that have an inherent relationship to the baptismal washing: first, the blessing of water, then the renunciation of sin by the elect, and their profession of faith. Following the baptismal washing, the effects received through this sacrament are given expression in the explanatory rites: the anointing with chrism (when confirmation does not immediately follow baptism), the clothing with a white garment, and the presentation of a lighted candle. [28] [33]

210   PRAYER OVER THE WATER: The celebration of baptism begins with the blessing of water, even when the sacraments of initiation are received outside the Easter season. Should the sacraments be celebrated outside the Easter Vigil but during the Easter season (see no. 26), the water blessed at the Vigil is used, but a prayer of thanksgiving, having the same themes as the blessing, is included. The blessing declares the religious meaning of water as God's creation and the sacramental use of water in the unfolding of the paschal mystery, and the blessing is also a remembrance of God's wonderful works in the history of salvation. [29] [210]

The blessing thus introduces an invocation of the Trinity at the very outset of the celebration of baptism. For it calls to mind the mystery of God's love from the beginning of the world and the creation of the human race; by invoking the Holy Spirit and proclaiming Christ's death and resurrection, it impresses on the mind the newness of Christian baptism, by which we share in his own death and resurrection and receive the holiness of God himself.

211   RENUNCIATION OF SIN AND PROFESSION OF FAITH: In their renunciation of sin and profession of faith those to be baptized express their explicit faith in the paschal mystery that has already been recalled in the blessing of water and that will be connoted by the words of the sacrament soon to be spoken by the baptizing minister. Adults are not saved unless they come forward of their own accord and with the will to accept God's gift through their own belief. The faith of those to be baptized is not simply the faith of the Church, [30] [211]

but the personal faith of each one of them and each one of them is expected to keep it a living faith.

Therefore the renunciation of sin and the profession of faith are an apt prelude to baptism, the sacrament of that faith by which the elect hold fast to God and receive new birth from him. Because of the renunciation of sin and the profession of faith, which form the one rite, the elect will not be baptized merely passively but will receive this great sacrament with the active resolve to renounce error and to hold fast to God. By their own personal act in the rite of renouncing sin and professing their faith, the elect as was prefigured in the first covenant with the patriarchs, renounce sin and Satan in order to commit themselves for ever to the promise of the Savior and to the mystery of the Trinity. By professing their faith before the celebrant and the entire community, the elect express the intention, developed to maturity during the preceding periods of initiation, to enter into a new covenant with Christ. Thus these adults embrace the faith that through divine help the Church has handed down, and are baptized in that faith.

212 BAPTISM: Immediately after their profession of living faith in Christ's paschal mystery, the elect come forward and receive that mystery as expressed in the washing with water; thus once the elect have professed faith in the Father, Son, and Holy Spirit, invoked by the celebrant, the divine persons act so that those they have chosen receive divine adoption and become members of the people of God.

213 Therefore in the celebration of baptism the washing with water should take on its full importance as the sign of that mystical sharing in Christ's death and resurrection through which those who believe in his name die to sin and rise to eternal life. Either immersion or the pouring of water should be chosen for the rite, whichever will serve in individual cases and in the various traditions and circumstances to ensure the clear understanding that this washing is not a mere purification rite but the sacrament of being joined to Christ.

214 EXPLANATORY RITES: The baptismal washing is followed by rites that give expression to the effects of the sacrament just received. The anointing with chrism is a sign of the royal priesthood of the baptized and that they are now numbered in the company of the people of God. The clothing with the baptismal garment signifies the new dignity they have received. The

presentation of a lighted candle shows that they are called to walk as befits the children of the light.

CELEBRATION OF CONFIRMATION

215   In accord with the ancient practice followed in the Roman liturgy, 34 adults are not to be baptized without receiving confirmation immediately afterward, unless some serious reason stands in the way. The conjunction of the two celebrations signifies the unity of the paschal mystery, the close link between the mission of the Son and the outpouring of the Holy Spirit, and the connection between the two sacraments through which the Son and the Holy Spirit come with the Father to those who are baptized.

216   Accordingly, confirmation is conferred after the explanatory rites of 35 baptism, the anointing after baptism (no. 228) being omitted.

THE NEOPHYTES' FIRST SHARING IN THE CELEBRATION OF THE EUCHARIST

217   Finally in the celebration of the eucharist, as they take part for the first 36 time and with full right, the newly baptized reach the culminating point in their Christian initiation. In this eucharist the neophytes, now raised to the ranks of the royal priesthood, have an active part both in the general intercessions and, to the extent possible, in bringing the gifts to the altar. With the entire community they share in the offering of the sacrifice and say the Lord's Prayer, giving expression to the spirit of adoption as God's children that they have received in baptism. When in communion they receive the body that was given for us and the blood that was shed, the neophytes are strengthened in the gifts they have already received and are given a foretaste of the eternal banquet.

OUTLINE OF THE RITE

SERVICE OF LIGHT

LITURGY OF THE WORD

CELEBRATION OF BAPTISM

Presentation of the Candidates
Invitation to Prayer
Litany of the Saints
Prayer over the Water
Profession of Faith
    Renunciation of Sin
    Profession of Faith
Baptism
Explanatory Rites
    [Anointing after Baptism]
    [Clothing with a Baptismal Garment]
    Presentation of a Lighted Candle

CELEBRATION OF CONFIRMATION

Invitation
Laying on of Hands
Anointing with Chrism

[RENEWAL OF BAPTISMAL PROMISES (AT THE EASTER VIGIL)]

Invitation
Renewal of Baptismal Promises
   Renunciation of Sin
   Profession of Faith
Sprinkling with Baptismal Water

LITURGY OF THE EUCHARIST

PERIOD OF POSTBAPTISMAL CATECHESIS OR MYSTAGOGY

244 The third step of Christian initiation, the celebration of the sacraments, 37 is followed by the final period, the period of postbaptismal catechesis or mystagogy. This is a time for the community and the neophytes together to grow in deepening their grasp of the paschal mystery and in making it part of their lives through meditation on the Gospel, sharing in the eucharist, and doing the works of charity. To strengthen the neophytes as they begin to walk in newness of life, the community of the faithful, their godparents, and their parish priests (pastors) should give them thoughtful and friendly help.

245 The neophytes are, as the term "mystagogy" suggests, introduced into 38 a fuller and more effective understanding of mysteries through the Gospel message they have learned and above all through their experience of the sacraments they have received. For they have truly been renewed in mind, tasted more deeply the sweetness of God's word, received the fellowship of the Holy Spirit, and grown to know the goodness of the Lord. Out of this experience, which belongs to Christians and increases as it is lived, they derive a new perception of the faith, of the Church, and of the world.

246 Just as their new participation in the sacraments enlightens the neo- 39 phytes' understanding of the Scriptures, so too it increases their contact with 235 the rest of the faithful and has an impact on the experience of the community.

As a result, interaction between the neophytes and the faithful is made easier and more beneficial. The period of postbaptismal catechesis is of great significance for both the neophytes and the rest of the faithful. Through it the neophytes, with the help of their godparents, should experience a full and joyful welcome into the community and enter into closer ties with the other faithful. The faithful, in turn, should derive from it a renewal of inspiration and of outlook.

247   Since the distinctive spirit and power of the period of postbaptismal catechesis or mystagogy derive from the new, personal experience of the sacraments and of the community, its main setting is the so-called Masses for neophytes, that is, the Sunday Masses of the Easter season. Besides being occasions for the newly baptized to gather with the community and share in the mysteries, these celebrations include particularly suitable readings from the Lectionary, especially the readings for Year A. Even when Christian initiation has been celebrated outside the usual times, the texts for these Sunday Masses of the Easter season may be used.

248   All the neophytes and their godparents should make an effort to take part in the Masses for the neophytes and the entire local community should be invited to participate with them. Special places in the congregation are to be reserved for the neophytes and their godparents. The homily and, as circumstances suggest, the general intercessions should take into account the presence and needs of the neophytes.

249   To close the period of postbaptismal catechesis, some sort of celebration should be held at the end of the Easter season near Pentecost Sunday; festivities in keeping with local custom may accompany the occasion.

250   On the anniversary of their baptism the neophytes should be brought together in order to give thanks to God, to share with one another their spiritual experiences, and to renew their commitment.

251   To show his pastoral concern for these new members of the Church, the bishop, particularly if he was unable to preside at the sacraments of initiation himself, should arrange, if possible, to meet the recently baptized at least once in the year and to preside at a celebration of the eucharist with them. At this Mass they may receive holy communion under both kinds.

PART II

RITES FOR PARTICULAR CIRCUMSTANCES

1 CHRISTIAN INITIATION OF CHILDREN WHO HAVE REACHED CATECHETICAL AGE

252   This form of the rite of Christian initiation is intended for children, 306 not baptized as infants, who have attained the use of reason and are of catechetical age. They seek Christian initiation either at the direction of their parents or guardians or, with parental permission, on their own initiative. Such children are capable of receiving and nurturing a personal faith and of recognizing an obligation in conscience. But they cannot yet be treated as adults because, at this stage of their lives, they are dependent on their parents or guardians and are still strongly influenced by their companions and their social surroundings.

253   The Christian initiation of these children requires both a conversion 307 that is personal and somewhat developed, in proportion to their age, and USA the assistance of the education they need. The process of initiation thus must be adapted both to their spiritual progress, that is, to the children's growth in faith, and to the catechetical instruction they receive. Accordingly, as with adults, their initiation is to be extended over several years, if need be, before they receive the sacraments. Also as with adults, their initiation is marked by several steps, the liturgical rites of acceptance into the order of catechumens (nos. 260–276), the optional rite of election (nos. 277–290), penitential rites or scrutinies (nos. 291–303), and the celebration of the sacraments of initiation (nos. 304–329); corresponding to the periods of adult initiation are the periods of the children's catechetical formation that lead up to and follow the steps of their initiation.

254   The children's progress in the formation they receive depends on the 308 help and example of their companions and on the influence of their parents. Both these factors should therefore be taken into account.

1. Since the children to be initiated often belong to a group of children of the same age who are already baptized and are preparing for confirmation and eucharist, their initiation progresses gradually and within the supportive setting of this group of companions.

2. It is to be hoped that the children will also receive as much help and example as possible from the parents, whose permission is required for the children to be initiated and to live the Christian life. The period of initiation will also provide a good opportunity for the family to have contact with priests and catechists.

255   For the celebrations proper to this form of Christian initiation, it is advantageous, as circumstances allow, to form a group of several children who are in this same situation, in order that by example they may help one another in their progress as catechumens.

256   In regard to the time for the celebration of the steps of initiation, it is preferable that, if possible, the final period of preparation, begun by the second step, the penitential rites (or by the optional rite of election), coincide with Lent and that the final step, celebration of the sacraments of initiation, take place at the Easter Vigil (see no. 8). Nevertheless before the children are admitted to the sacraments at Easter, it should be established that they are ready for the sacraments. Celebration at this time must also be consistent with the program of catechetical instruction they are receiving, since the candidates should, if possible, come to the sacraments of initiation at the time that their baptized companions are to receive confirmation or eucharist.

257   For children of this age, at the rites during the process of initiation, it is generally preferable not to have the whole parish community present, but simply represented. Thus these rites should be celebrated with the active participation of a congregation that consists of a suitable number of the faithful, the parents, family, members of the catechetical group, and a few adult friends.

258   Each conference of bishops may adapt and add to the form of the rite given here in order that the rite will more effectively satisfy local needs conditions, and pastoral requirements. [The National Conference of Catholic Bishops has done this by providing an optional "Rite of Election" before "Second Step: Penitential Rites (Scrutinies)."] The rites for the presentation of the Creed (nos. 157–162) and the Lord's Prayer (nos. 178–183), adapted to the age of the children, may be incorporated. When the form of the rite of initiation for children is translated, the instructions and prayers should be adapted to their understanding. Furthermore, in addition to any liturgica

text translated from the Latin *editio typica,* the conference of bishops may also approve an original, alternative text that says the same thing in a way more suited to children (see *Christian Initiation,* General Introduction, no. 32).

259   In following this form of the rite of Christian initiation the celebrant should make full and wise use of the options mentioned in *Christian Initiation,* General Introduction (nos. 34–35), in the *Rite of Baptism for Children,* Introduction (no. 31), and in the *Rite of Christian Initiation of Adults,* Introduction (no. 35). 313

FIRST STEP: ACCEPTANCE INTO THE ORDER OF CATECHUMENS

260   It is important that this rite be celebrated with an actively participating but small congregation, since the presence of a large group might make the children uncomfortable (see no. 257). When possible, the children's parents or guardians should be present. If they cannot come, they should indicate that they have given consent to their children and their place should be taken by "sponsors" (see no. 10), that is, suitable members of the Church who act on this occasion for the parents and present the children. The presiding celebrant is a priest or deacon. 314

261   The celebration takes place in the church or in a place that, according to the age and understanding of the children, can help them to experience a warm welcome. As circumstances suggest, the first part of the rite, "Receiving the Children," is carried out at the entrance of the place chosen for the celebration, and the second part of the rite, "Liturgy of the Word," takes place inside. 315 329

The celebration is not normally combined with celebration of the eucharist.

OUTLINE OF THE RITE

RECEIVING THE CHILDREN

Greeting
Opening Dialogue
Affirmation by the Parents (Sponsors)
    and the Assembly
Signing of the Candidates with the Cross
    Signing of the Forehead
    [Signing of the Other Senses]
Invitation to the Celebration of the Word of God

LITURGY OF THE WORD

Instruction
Readings
Homily
[Presentation of a Bible]
Intercessions for the Children
Prayer over the Children
Dismissal

74

RITE OF ELECTION OR ENROLLMENT OF NAMES [OPTIONAL]

277   The (optional) liturgical rite called both election and the enrollment of names may be celebrated with children of catechetical age, especially those whose catechumenate has extended over a long period of time. This celebration, which usually coincides with the beginning of Lent, marks the beginning of the period of final preparation for the sacraments of initiation, during which the children will be encouraged to follow Christ with greater generosity.

278   In the rite of election, on the basis of the testimony of parents, god-parents and catechists and of the children's reaffirmation of their intention, the Church judges their state of readiness and decides on their advancement toward the sacraments of initiation. Thus the Church makes its "election," that is, the choice and admission of those children who have the dispositions that make them fit to take part, at the next major celebration, in the sacraments of initiation.

279   The rite should take place in the cathedral church, in a parish church or, if necessary, in some other suitable and fitting place. If the election of children of catechetical age is to take place within a celebration in which older catechumens are also to receive the Church's election, the rite for adults (nos. 129–137) should be used, with appropriate adaptation of the texts to be made by the celebrant.

280   The rite is celebrated within Mass, after the homily, and should be celebrated within the Mass of the First Sunday of Lent. If, for pastoral reasons, the rite is celebrated on a different day, the texts and the readings of the ritual Mass "Christian Initiation: Election or Enrollment of Names" may always be used. When the Mass of the day is celebrated and its readings are not suitable, the readings are those given for the First Sunday of Lent or others may be chosen from elsewhere in the Lectionary.

When celebrated outside Mass, the rite takes place after the readings and the homily and is concluded with the dismissal of both the elect and the faithful.

OUTLINE OF THE RITE

LITURGY OF THE WORD

Homily
Presentation of the Catechumens
Affirmation by the Parents, Godparents,
 [and the Assembly]
Invitation and Enrollment of Names
Act of Admission or Election
[Recognition of the Godparent(s)]
Intercessions for the Elect
Prayer over the Elect
Dismissal of the Elect

LITURGY OF THE EUCHARIST

SECOND STEP: PENITENTIAL RITES (SCRUTINIES)

291 These penitential rites, which mark the second step in the children's 330 Christian initiation, are major occasions in their catechumenate. They are held within a celebration of the word of God as a kind of scrutiny, similar to the scrutinies in the adult rite. Thus the guidelines given for the adult rite (nos. 141–146) may be followed and adapted, since the children's penitential rites have a similar purpose.

292 Because the penitential rites normally belong to the period of final 331 preparation for baptism, the condition for their celebration is that the children are approaching the maturity of faith and understanding requisite for baptism.

293 Along with the children, their godparents and their baptized compan- 332 ions from the catechetical group participate in the celebration of these penitential rites. Therefore the rites are to be adapted in such a way that they also benefit the participants who are not catechumens. In particular, these penitential rites are a proper occasion for baptized children of the catechetical group to celebrate the sacrament of penance for the first time. When this is the case, care should be taken to include explanations, prayers, and ritual acts that relate to the celebration of the sacrament with these children.

294 The penitential rites are celebrated during Lent, if the catechumens 333 are to be initiated at Easter; if not, at the most suitable time. At least one penitential rite is to be celebrated, and, if this can be arranged conveniently, a second should follow after an appropriate interval. The texts for a second celebration are to be composed on the model of the first given here, but the texts for the intercessions and prayer of exorcism given in the adult rite (nos. 153–154, 167–168, 174–175) are used, with the requisite modifications.

OUTLINE OF THE RITE

LITURGY OF THE WORD

Greeting and Introduction
Prayer
Readings
Homily
Intercessions
Exorcism
Anointing with the Oil of Catechumens
   [or Laying on of Hands]
Dismissal of the Children

LITURGY OF PENANCE

THIRD STEP: CELEBRATION OF THE SACRAMENTS OF INITIATION

304   In order to bring out the paschal character of baptism, celebration of 343 the sacraments of initiation should preferably take place at the Easter Vigil or on a Sunday, the day that the Church devotes to the remembrance of Christ's resurrection (see *Rite of Baptism for Children,* Introduction, no. 9). But the provisions of no. 256 should also guide the choice of time for the celebration of the sacraments of initiation.

305   At this third step of their Christian initiation, the children will receive 344 the sacrament of baptism, the bishop or priest who baptizes them will also confer confirmation, and the children will for the first time participate in the liturgy of the eucharist.

306   If the sacraments of initiation are celebrated at a time other than the 345 Easter Vigil or Easter Sunday, the Mass of the day or one of the ritual Masses in the Roman Missal, "Christian Initiation: Baptism" is used. The readings are chosen from those given in the Lectionary for Mass, "Celebration of the Sacraments of Initiation apart from the Easter Vigil"; but the readings for the Sunday or feast on which the celebration takes place may be used instead.

307   All the children to be baptized are to be accompanied by their own 346 godparent or godparents, chosen by themselves and approved by the priest (see no. 11; *Christian Initiation,* General Introduction, no. 10).

308   Baptized children of the catechetical group may be completing their Christian initiation in the sacraments of confirmation and the eucharist at this same celebration. When the bishop himself will not be the celebrant, he should grant the faculty to confirm such children to the priest who will be the celebrant.[1] For their confirmation, previously baptized children of the catechetical group are to have their own sponsors. If possible, these should be the persons who were godparents for their baptism, but other qualified persons may be chosen.[2]

---

[1] See *Rite of Confirmation,* Introduction, no. 7.b.

[2] See ibid., nos. 5 and 6.

OUTLINE OF THE RITE

LITURGY OF THE WORD

CELEBRATION OF BAPTISM

Invitation to Prayer
Prayer over the Water
[Community's Profession of Faith]
Children's Profession of Faith
    Renunciation of Sin
    [Anointing with the Oil of Catechumens]
    Profession of Faith
Baptism
Explanatory Rites
    [Anointing after Baptism]
    [Clothing with a Baptismal Garment]
    Presentation of a Lighted Candle

CELEBRATION OF CONFIRMATION

Invitation
Laying on of Hands
Anointing with Chrism

LITURGY OF THE EUCHARIST

80

PERIOD OF POSTBAPTISMAL CATECHESIS OR MYSTAGOGY

330 A period of postbaptismal catechesis or mystagogy should be provided 369 to assist the young neophytes and their companions who have completed their Christian initiation. This period can be arranged by an adaptation of the guidelines given for adults (nos. 244–251).

2 CHRISTIAN INITIATION OF ADULTS IN EXCEPTIONAL CIRCUMSTANCES

331 Exceptional circumstances may arise in which the local bishop, in 240 individual cases, can allow the use of a form of Christian initiation that is simpler than the usual, complete rite (see no. 34.4).

The bishop may permit this simpler form to consist in the abbreviated form of the rite (nos. 340–369) that is carried out in one celebration. Or he may permit an expansion of this abbreviated rite, so that there are celebrations not only of the sacraments of initiation but also of one or more of the rites belonging to the period of the catechumenate and to the period of purification and enlightenment (see nos. 332–335).

The extraordinary circumstances in question are either events that prevent the candidate from completing all the steps of the catechumenate or a depth of Christian conversion and a degree of religious maturity that lead the local bishop to decide that the candidate may receive baptism without delay.

EXPANDED FORM

332 Extraordinary circumstances, for example, sickness, old age, change 274 of residence, long absence for travel, may sometimes either prevent a candidate from celebrating the rite of acceptance that leads to the period of the catechumenate or, having begun the catechumenate, from completing it by participation in all the rites belonging to the period. Yet merely to use the abbreviated form of the rite given in nos. 340–369 could mean a spiritual loss for the candidate, who would be deprived of the benefits of a longer preparation for the sacraments of initiation. It is therefore important that,

81

with the bishop's permission, an expanded form of initiation be developed by the incorporation of elements from the complete rite for the Christian initiation of adults.

333   Through such an expansion of the abbreviated rite a new candidate can reach the same level as those who are already advanced in the catechumenate, since some of the earlier elements from the full rite can be added, for example, the rite of acceptance into the order of catechumens (nos. 48–74) or the minor exorcisms (no. 94) and blessings (no. 97) from the period of the catechumenate. The expansion also makes it possible for a candidate who had begun the catechumenate with others, but was forced to interrupt it, to complete the catechumenate alone by celebrating, in addition to the sacraments of initiation (see nos. 206–217), elements from the full rite, for example, the rite of election (see nos. 118–128) and rites belonging to the period of purification and enlightenment (see nos. 141–149).

334   Pastors can arrange this expanded form of initiation by taking the abbreviated form as a basis, then choosing wisely from the full rite to make adaptations in any of the following ways:

1. supplementing the abbreviated form: for example, adding rites belonging to the period of the catechumenate (nos. 81–103) or adding the presentations (nos. 157–162, 178–182);

2. making the rite of "Receiving the Candidate" or the "Liturgy of the Word" in the abbreviated rite separate or expanded celebrations. As to "Receiving the Candidate" (nos. 340–345), this can be expanded by replacing no. 342 and using elements from the rite of acceptance into the order of catechumens (nos. 48–74); or, depending on the candidate's state of preparation, by celebrating the rite of election (nos. 129–137) in place of nos. 343–344. As to the "Liturgy of the Word," after the readings, the intercessions, penitential rite, and prayer of exorcism, nos. 349–351, can be adapted by use of the elements in the scrutinies (nos. 152–154, 166–168, 173–175).

3. replacing elements of the complete rite with elements of the abbreviated form; or combining the rite of acceptance into the order of catechumens (nos. 48–74) and the rite of election (nos. 129–137) at the time of receiving a properly disposed candidate (which is comparable to the

time of receiving interested inquirers in the period of the precatechumenate; see no. 39.3).

335   When this expanded form of initiation is arranged, care should be 277 taken to ensure that:

1. the candidate has received a full catechesis;

2. the rite is celebrated with the active participation of an assembly;

3. after receiving the sacraments the neophyte has the benefit of a period of postbaptismal catechesis, if at all possible.

ABBREVIATED FORM

336   Before the abbreviated form of the rite is celebrated the candidate 241 must have gone through an adequate period of instruction and preparation before baptism, in order to purify his or her motives for requesting baptism and to grow stronger in conversion and faith. The candidate should also have chosen godparents or a godparent (see no. 11) and become acquainted with the local Christian community (see nos. 39, 75.2).

337   This rite includes elements that express the presentation and welcom- 242 ing of the candidate and that also express the candidate's clear and firm resolve to request Christian initiation, as well as the Church's approval of the candidate. A suitable liturgy of the word is also celebrated, then the sacraments of initiation.

338   Normally the rite is celebrated within Mass. The choice of readings 243 should be in keeping with the character of the celebration; they may be either those of the day or those in the Lectionary for Mass, ritual Mass, "Christian Initiation apart from the Easter Vigil." The other Mass texts are those of one of the ritual Masses "Christian Initiation: Baptism" or of another Mass. After receiving baptism and confirmation, the candidate takes part for the first time in the celebration of the eucharist.

339   If at all possible, the celebration should take place on a Sunday 244 (see no. 27), with the local community taking an active part.

OUTLINE OF THE RITE

RECEIVING THE CANDIDATE

Greeting
Opening Dialogue
Candidate's Declaration
Affirmation by the Godparents
Invitation to the Celebration of the Word of God

LITURGY OF THE WORD

Readings
Homily
Intercessions for the Candidate
[Penitential Rite]
Prayer of Exorcism
Anointing with the Oil of Catechumens
   or Laying on of Hands

CELEBRATION OF BAPTISM

Invitation to Prayer
Prayer over the Water
Profession of Faith
   Renunciation of Sin
   Profession of Faith
Baptism
Explanatory Rites

[Clothing with a Baptismal Garment]
Presentation of a Lighted Candle

CELEBRATION OF CONFIRMATION

Invitation
Laying on of Hands
Anointing with Chrism

LITURGY OF THE EUCHARIST

3 CHRISTIAN INITIATION OF A PERSON IN DANGER OF DEATH

370   Persons, whether catechumens or not, who are in danger of death but   278
are not at the point of death and so are able to hear and answer the questions
involved may be baptized with this short rite.

371   Persons who have already been accepted as catechumens must make   279
a promise that upon recovery they will complete the usual catechesis. Persons
who are not catechumens must give serious indication of their conversion
to Christ and renunciation of pagan worship and must not be seen to be
attached to anything that conflicts with the moral life (for example, "simul-
taneous polygamy"). They must also promise that upon recovery they will
go through the complete program of initiation as it applies to them.

372   This shorter rite is designed particularly for use by catechists and   280
laypersons; a priest or a deacon may use it in a case of emergency. But
normally a priest or a deacon is to use the abbreviated form of Christian
initiation given in nos. 340–369, making any changes required by circumstances of place and time.
     The minister of baptism who is a priest should, when the chrism is at hand
and there is time, confer confirmation after the baptism; in this case there
is no postbaptismal anointing.
     The minister of baptism who is a priest, a deacon, or a catechist or layperson

having permission to distribute communion, should, if this is possible, give the eucharist to the newly baptized person. In this case before the beginning of the celebration of the rite the blessed sacrament is placed reverently on a table covered with a white cloth.

373   In the case of a person who is at the point of death, that is, whose death is imminent, and time is short, the minister, omitting everything else, pours natural water (even if not blessed) on the head of the sick person, while saying the usual sacramental form (see *Christian Initiation,* General Introduction, no. 23).

374   If persons who were baptized when in danger of death or at the point of death recover their health, they are to be given a suitable formation, be welcomed at the church in due time, and there receive the other sacraments of initiation. In such cases the guidelines given in nos. 400–410 for baptized but uncatechized adults are followed, with the necessary changes. The same guidelines should be applied when sick persons recover after receiving not only baptism but also confirmation and eucharist as viaticum.

OUTLINE OF THE RITE

INTRODUCTORY RITES

Opening Dialogue
Affirmation by the Godparent and Witnesses

LITURGY OF THE WORD

Gospel Reading
Intercessions for the Candidate
Prayer over the Candidate

CELEBRATION OF BAPTISM

Renunciation of Sin
Profession of Faith
Baptism
[Anointing after Baptism]

CELEBRATION OF CONFIRMATION

Invitation
Laying on of Hands
Anointing with Chrism

CELEBRATION OF VIATICUM

Invitation to Prayer
Communion as Viaticum

Prayer after Communion

CONCLUDING RITES

Blessing
Sign of Peace

4 PREPARATION OF UNCATECHIZED ADULTS FOR CONFIRMATION AND EUCHARIST

400   The following pastoral guidelines concern adults who were baptized 2
as infants either as Roman Catholics or as members of another Christian U
community but did not receive further catechetical formation nor, consequently, the sacraments of confirmation and eucharist. These suggestions
may also be applied to similar cases, especially that of an adult who recovers
after being baptized in danger of death or at the point of death (see no. 374).
   Even though uncatechized adults have not yet heard the message of the
mystery of Christ, their status differs from that of catechumens, since by
baptism they have already become members of the Church and children of
God. Hence their conversion is based on the baptism they have already
received, the effects of which they must develop.

401   As in the case of catechumens, the preparation of these adults requires
a considerable time (see no. 76), during which the faith infused in baptism
must grow in them and take deep root through the pastoral formation they
receive. A program of training, catechesis suited to their needs, contact with
the community of the faithful, and participation in certain liturgical rites are
needed in order to strengthen them in the Christian life.

402   For the most part the plan of catechesis corresponds to the one laid
down for catechumens (see no. 75.1). But in the process of catechesis the
priest, deacon, or catechist should take into account that these adults have
a special status because they are already baptized.

403   Just as it helps catechumens, the Christian community should also help

these adults by its love and prayer (see nos. 4, 75.2) and by testifying to their suitability when it is time for them to be admitted to the sacraments (see nos. 120, 121).

404 A sponsor presents these adults to the community (see no. 10). During 299 the period of their catechetical formation, they all choose godparents (a godfather, a godmother, or both) approved by the priest. Their godparents work with these adults as the representatives of the community and have the same responsibilities as the godparents have toward catechumens (see no. 11). The same persons who were the godparents at the baptism of these adults may be chosen as godparents at this time, provided they are truly capable of carrying out the responsibilities of godparents.

405 The period of preparation is made holy by means of liturgical cele- 300 brations. The first of these is a rite by which the adults are welcomed into USA the community and acknowledge themselves to be part of it because they have already been marked with the seal of baptism. [The Rite of Welcoming the Candidates, which follows in Part II, 4A is provided for this purpose.]

406 Once a rite of reception has been celebrated, these adults take part 301 in celebrations of the word of God, both those of the entire Christian assembly and those celebrations arranged specially for the benefit of the catechumens (see nos. 81–84).

407 As a sign of God's activity in this work of preparation, some of the 302 rites belonging to the catechumenate, especially suited to the condition and USA spiritual needs of these baptized adults, can be used to advantage. Among these are the presentation of the Creed (nos. 157–162) and of the Lord's Prayer (nos. 178–182) or also a presentation of a book of the Gospels (no. 64). [The additional rites in Part II, 4B, 4C, and 4D may also be used in accordance with the individual needs and circumstances of the candidates.]

408 The period of catechesis for these adults should be properly coordi- 303 nated with the liturgical year. This is particularly true of its final phase, which should as a rule coincide with Lent. During the Lenten season penitential services should be arranged in such a way as to prepare these adults for the celebration of the sacrament of penance.

409   The high point of their entire formation will normally be the Easter 3⬤
Vigil. At that time they will make a profession of the faith in which they were
baptized, receive the sacrament of confirmation, and take part in the eucharist.
If, because neither the bishop nor another authorized minister is present,
confirmation cannot be given at the Easter Vigil, it is to be celebrated as
soon as possible and, if this can be arranged, during the Easter season.

410   These adults will complete their Christian formation and become fully 3⬤
integrated into the community by going through the period of postbaptismal
catechesis or mystagogy with the newly baptized members of the Christian
community.

OPTIONAL RITES FOR BAPTIZED BUT UNCATECHIZED ADULTS

4A RITE OF WELCOMING THE CANDIDATES

411   This optional rite welcomes baptized but previously uncatechized adults
who are seeking to complete their Christian initiation through the sacraments
of confirmation and eucharist or to be received into the full communion of
the Catholic Church.

412   The prayers and ritual gestures acknowledge that such candidates are
already part of the community because they have been marked by baptism.
Now the Church surrounds them with special care and support as they
prepare to be sealed with the gift of the Spirit in confirmation and take their
place at the banquet table of Christ's sacrifice.

413   Once formally welcomed into the life of the community, these adults,
besides regularly attending Sunday eucharist, take part in celebrations of the
word of God in the full Christian assembly and in celebrations arranged
especially for the benefit of the candidates.

414   The rite will take place on specified days throughout the year (see no. 18) that are suited to local conditions.

415   When the rite of welcoming candidates for the sacraments of confirmation and eucharist is to be combined with the rite of acceptance into the order of catechumens, the alternate rite found in the RCIA, Appendix I, 1 is used.

OUTLINE OF THE RITE

WELCOMING THE CANDIDATES

Greeting
Opening Dialogue
Candidates' Declaration of Intent
Affirmation by the Sponsors and the Assembly
Signing of the Candidates with the Cross
   Signing of the Forehead
   [Signing of the Other Senses]
   Concluding Prayer

LITURGY OF THE WORD

Instruction
Readings
Homily
[Presentation of a Bible]
Profession of Faith
General Intercessions
Prayer over the Candidates
[Dismissal of the Assembly]

LITURGY OF THE EUCHARIST

4B RITE OF SENDING THE CANDIDATES FOR RECOGNITION BY THE BISHOP AND FOR THE CALL TO CONTINUING CONVERSION

434　This optional rite is provided for parishes whose candidates seeking to complete their Christian initiation or to be received into the full communion of the Catholic Church will be recognized by the bishop in a subsequent celebration (for example, at the cathedral with the bishop).

435　Because he is the sign of unity within the particular Church, it is fitting for the bishop to recognize these candidates. It is the responsibility of the parish community, however, to prepare the candidates for their fuller life in the Church. Through the experience of worship, daily life, and service in the parish community the candidates deepen their appreciation of the Church's tradition and universal character.

　　This rite offers that local community the opportunity to express its joy in the candidates' decision and to send them forth to the celebration of recognition assured of the parish's care and support.

436　The rite is celebrated in the parish church at a suitable time prior to the rite of recognition and call to continuing conversion.

437　When the rite of sending candidates for recognition is to be combined with the rite of sending catechumens for election, the alternate rite found in the RCIA (Appendix I, 2) is used.

OUTLINE OF THE RITE

LITURGY OF THE WORD

Homily
Presentation of the Candidates
Affirmation by the Sponsors [and the Assembly]
General Intercessions
Prayer over the Candidates
[Dismissal of the Assembly]

LITURGY OF THE EUCHARIST

4c RITE OF CALLING THE CANDIDATES TO CONTINUING CONVERSION

446 This rite may be celebrated with baptized but previously uncatechized adults who wish to complete their Christian initiation through the sacraments of confirmation and eucharist or who wish to be received into the full communion of the Catholic Church.

447 The rite is intended for celebrations in communities where there are no catechumens.

448 The rite is celebrated at the beginning of Lent. The presiding celebrant is the pastor of the parish.

449 If the calling of candidates to continuing conversion is to be combined with the rite of election of catechumens (either in a parish celebration or at one in which the bishop is celebrant) the alternate rite found in the RCIA (Appendix I, 3) is used.

OUTLINE OF THE RITE

LITURGY OF THE WORD

Homily
Presentation of the Candidates for
    Confirmation and Eucharist
Affirmation by the Sponsors [and the Assembly]
Act of Recognition
General Intercessions
Prayer over the Candidates
[Dismissal of the Assembly]

LITURGY OF THE EUCHARIST

4D PENITENTIAL RITE (SCRUTINY)

459   This penitential rite can serve to mark the Lenten purification of baptized but previously uncatechized adults who are preparing to receive the sacraments of confirmation and eucharist or to be received into the full communion of the Catholic Church. It is held within a celebration of the word of God as a kind of scrutiny, similar to the scrutinies for catechumens.

460   Because the penitential rite normally belongs to the period of final preparation for the sacraments, its celebration presumes that the candidates are approaching the maturity of faith and understanding requisite for fuller life in the community.

461   Along with the candidates, their sponsors and the larger liturgical assembly also participate in the celebration of the penitential rite. Therefore the rite is to be adapted in such a way that it benefits all the participants. This penitential rite may also help to prepare the candidates to celebrate the sacrament of penance.

462   This penitential rite may be celebrated on the Second Sunday of Lent or on a Lenten weekday, if the candidates are to receive the sacraments of confirmation and eucharist and/or be received into the full communion of the Catholic Church at Easter; if not, at the most suitable time.

463   This penitential rite is intended solely for celebrations with baptized adults preparing for confirmation and eucharist or reception into the full communion of the Catholic Church. Because the prayer of exorcism in the three scrutinies for catechumens who have received the Church's election properly belongs to the elect and uses numerous images referring to their approaching baptism, those scrutinies of the elect and this penitential rite for those preparing for confirmation and eucharist have been kept separate and distinct. Thus, no combined rite has been included in Appendix I.

OUTLINE OF THE RITE

INTRODUCTORY RITES

Greeting and Introduction
Prayer

LITURGY OF THE WORD

Readings
Homily
Invitation to Silent Prayer
Intercessions for the Candidates
Prayer over the Candidates
[Dismissal of the Assembly]

LITURGY OF THE EUCHARIST

5 RECEPTION OF BAPTIZED CHRISTIANS INTO THE FULL COMMUNION OF THE CATHOLIC CHURCH

473   This is the liturgical rite by which a person born and baptized in a R1
separated ecclesial Community is received, according to the Latin rite,[1] into
the full communion of the Catholic Church. The rite is so arranged that no
greater burden than necessary (see Acts 15:28) is required for the estab-
lishment of communion and unity.[2]

474   In the case of Eastern Christians who enter into the fullness of Catholic R2
communion, no liturgical rite is required, but simply a profession of Catholic
faith, even if such persons are permitted, in virtue of recourse to the Apostolic
See, to transfer to the Latin rite.[3]

475   In regard to the manner of celebrating the rite of reception: R3

1. The rite should appear clearly as a celebration of the Church and have
as its high point eucharistic communion. For this reason the rite should
normally take place within Mass.

2. Any appearance of triumphalism should be carefully avoided and the
manner of celebrating this Mass should be decided beforehand and with
a view to the particular circumstances. Both the ecumenical implications
and the bond between the candidate and the parish community should
be considered. Often it will be preferable to celebrate the Mass with only
a few relatives and friends. If for a serious reason Mass cannot be celebrated,
the reception should at least take place within a liturgy of the word,
whenever this is possible. The person to be received into full communion
should be consulted about the form of reception.

---

[1] See Vatican Council II, Constitution on the Liturgy *Sacrosanctum Concilium*, art. 69, b;
Decree on Ecumenism *Unitatis redintegratio*, no. 3. Secretariat for Christian Unity, *Ecumenical Directory I*, no. 19; AAS 59 (1967), 581.
[2] See Vatican Council II, Decree on Ecumenism *Unitatis redintegratio*, no. 18.
[3] See Vatican Council II, Decree on the Eastern Catholic Churches *Orientalium Ecclesiarum*,
nos. 25 and 4.

476   If the rite of reception is celebrated outside Mass, the Mass in which R
for the first time the newly received will take part with the Catholic community should be celebrated as soon as possible, in order to make clear the
connection between the reception and eucharistic communion.

477   The baptized Christian is to receive both doctrinal and spiritual prep- ₨
aration, adapted to individual pastoral requirements, for reception into the
full communion of the Catholic Church. The candidate should learn to deepen
an inner adherence to the Church, where he or she will find the fullness of
his or her baptism. During the period of preparation the candidate may share
in worship in conformity with the provisions of the *Ecumenical Directory.*
   Anything that would equate candidates for reception with those who are
catechumens is to be absolutely avoided.

478   During the period of their doctrinal and spiritual preparation individual ▶
candidates for reception into the full communion of the Catholic Church
may benefit from the celebration of liturgical rites marking their progress in
formation. Thus, for pastoral reasons and in light of the catechesis in the
faith which these baptized Christians have received previously, one or several
of the rites included in Part II, "4 Preparation of Uncatechized Adults for
Confirmation and Eucharist," may be celebrated as they are presented or in
similar words. In all cases, however, discernment should be made regarding
the length of catechetical formation required for each individual candidate
for reception into the full communion of the Catholic Church.

479   One who was born and baptized outside the visible communion of
the Catholic Church is not required to make an abjuration of heresy, but
simply a profession of faith.[4]

480   The sacrament of baptism cannot be repeated and therefore it is not
permitted to confer it again conditionally, unless there is a reasonable doubt
about the fact or validity of the baptism already conferred. If serious investigation raises such prudent doubt and it seems necessary to confer baptism
again conditionally, the minister should explain beforehand the reasons why
this is being done and a nonsolemn form of baptism is to be used.[5]

---

[4] See Secretariat for Christian Unity, *Ecumenical Directory I,* nos. 19 and 20: AAS 59 (1967),
581.
[5] See ibid., nos. 14-15: AAS 59 (1967), 580.

The local Ordinary is to decide in each case what rites are to be included or excluded in conferring conditional baptism.

481   It is the office of the bishop to receive baptized Christians into the full communion of the Catholic Church. But a priest to whom the bishop entrusts the celebration of the rite has the faculty of confirming the candidate within the rite of reception,[6] unless the person received has already been validly confirmed. R8

482   If the profession of faith and reception take place within Mass, the candidate, according to his or her own conscience, should make a confession of sins beforehand, first informing the confessor that he or she is about to be received into full communion. Any confessor who is lawfully approved may hear the candidate's confession. R9

483   At the reception, the candidate should be accompanied by a sponsor and may even have two sponsors. If someone has had the principal part in guiding or preparing the candidate, he or she should be the sponsor. R10

484   In the eucharistic celebration within which reception into full communion takes place or, if the reception takes place outside Mass, in the Mass that follows at a later time, communion under both kinds is permitted for the person received, the sponsor, the parents and spouse who are Catholics, lay catechists who may have instructed the person, and, if the number involved and other circumstances make this feasible, for all Catholics present. R11

485   The conferences of bishops may, in accord with the provisions of the Constitution on the Liturgy, art. 63, adapt the rite of reception to various circumstances. The local Ordinary, by expanding or shortening the rite, may arrange it to suit the particular circumstances of the persons and place involved.[7] R12

486   The names of those received into the full communion of the Catholic Church should be recorded in a special book, with the date and place of their baptism also noted. R13

---

[6] See *Rite of Confirmation,* Introduction, no. 7. b.
[7] See Secretariat for Christian Unity, *Ecumenical Directory I,* no. 19: AAS 59 (1967), 581.

OUTLINE OF THE RITE

LITURGY OF THE WORD

Readings
Homily

CELEBRATION OF RECEPTION

Invitation
Profession of Faith
Act of Reception
[Confirmation]
    Laying on of Hands
    Anointing with Chrism
Celebrant's Sign of Welcome
General Intercessions
Sign of Peace

LITURGY OF THE EUCHARIST

RECEPTION OUTSIDE MASS

499   If, for a serious reason, the rite of reception into full communion takes R22 place outside Mass, a liturgy of the word is to be celebrated.

[If, in exceptional circumstances, not even a liturgy of the word is possible, R28 just the celebration of reception itself takes place as described in nos. 490– 497. It begins with introductory words in which the celebrant quotes from Scripture, for example, a text in praise of the mercy of God that has guided the candidate, and speaks of the eucharistic communion that will follow on the earliest day possible.]

500   The celebrant, vested in alb, or at least surplice, with a stole of festive R23 color, greets those present.

501   A suitable song may be sung, then there are one or more readings R24 from Scripture, which the celebrant explains in the homily (see no. 489). The readings may be chosen from those provided in the Lectionary for Mass for the day, for the ritual Mass "Christian Initiation apart from the Easter Vigil," or for the Mass "For the Unity of Christians"; but they are preferably chosen from those listed here, as indicated for the rite of reception into full communion.

APPENDIX

ADDITIONAL (COMBINED) RITES

1 CELEBRATION OF THE RITE OF ACCEPTANCE INTO THE ORDER OF CATECHUMENS AND OF THE RITE OF WELCOMING BAPTIZED BUT PREVIOUSLY UNCATECHIZED ADULTS WHO ARE PREPARING FOR CONFIRMATION AND/OR EUCHARIST OR RECEPTION INTO THE FULL COMMUNION OF THE CATHOLIC CHURCH

505   This rite is for use in communities where catechumens are preparing for initiation and where baptized but previously uncatechized adults are beginning catechetical formation either prior to completing their Christian initiation in the sacraments of confirmation and eucharist or prior to being received into the full communion of the Catholic Church.

506   In the catechesis of the community and in the celebration of these rites, care must be taken to maintain the distinction between the catechumens and the baptized candidates.

OUTLINE OF THE RITE

RECEIVING THE CANDIDATES

Greeting
Opening Dialogue with Candidates for the
   Catechumenate and with the Candidates for
      Post-baptismal Catechesis
Catechumens' First Acceptance of the Gospel
Candidates' Declaration of Intent
Affirmation by the Sponsors and the Assembly
Signing of the Catechumens and
   of the Candidates with the Cross
   Signing of the Forehead of the Catechumens
   [Signing of the Other Senses
     of the Catechumens]
   Signing of the Forehead of the Candidates
   [Signing of the Other Senses
     of the Candidates]
   Concluding Prayer
Invitation to the Celebration of the Word of God

LITURGY OF THE WORD

Instruction
Readings
Homily
[Presentation of a Bible]
Intercessions for the Catechumens and Candidates
Prayer over the Catechumens and Candidates
Dismissal of the Catechumens

LITURGY OF THE EUCHARIST

2 PARISH CELEBRATION FOR SENDING CATECHUMENS FOR ELECTION AND CANDIDATES FOR RECOGNITION BY THE BISHOP [OPTIONAL]

530   This optional rite is provided for parishes whose catechumens will celebrate their election and whose adult candidates for confirmation and eucharist or reception into the full communion of the Catholic Church will celebrate their recognition in a subsequent celebration (for example, at the cathedral with the bishop).

531   As the focal point of the Church's concern for the catechumens, admission to election belongs to the bishop who is usually its presiding celebrant. It is within the parish community, however, that the preliminary judgment is made concerning the catechumens' state of formation and progress.

   This rite offers that local community the opportunity to express its approval of the catechumens and to send them forth to the celebration of election assured of the parish's care and support.

532   In addition, those who either are completing their initiation through the sacraments of confirmation and the eucharist or are preparing for reception into the full communion of the Catholic Church are also included in this rite, since they too will be presented to the bishop at the celebration of the rite of election for the catechumens.

533   The rite is celebrated in the parish church at a suitable time prior to the rite of election.

534   The rite takes place after the homily in a celebration of the word of God (see no. 89) or at Mass.

535   In the catechesis of the community and in the celebration of these rites, care must be taken to maintain the distinction between the catechumens and the baptized candidates.

OUTLINE OF THE RITE

LITURGY OF THE WORD

Homily
Presentation of the Catechumens
Affirmation by the Godparents
  [and the Assembly]
Presentation of the Candidates
Affirmation by the Sponsors
  [and the Assembly]
Intercessions for the Catechumens
  and Candidates
Prayer over the Catechumens
  and Candidates
Dismissal of the Catechumens

LITURGY OF THE EUCHARIST

3 CELEBRATION OF THE RITE OF ELECTION OF CATECHUMENS AND OF THE CALL TO CONTINUING CONVERSION OF CANDIDATES WHO ARE PREPARING FOR CONFIRMATION AND/OR EUCHARIST OR RECEPTION INTO THE FULL COMMUNION OF THE CATHOLIC CHURCH

547 This rite is for use when the election of catechumens and the call to continuing conversion of candidates preparing either for confirmation and/or eucharist or reception into the full communion of the Catholic Church are celebrated together.

548 The rite should normally take place on the First Sunday of Lent, and the presiding celebrant is the bishop or his delegate.

549 In the catechesis of the community and in the celebration of these rites, care must be taken to maintain the distinction between the catechumens and the baptized candidates.

OUTLINE OF THE RITE

LITURGY OF THE WORD

Homily

CELEBRATION OF ELECTION

Presentation of the Catechumens
Affirmation by the Godparents [and the Assembly]
Invitation and Enrollment of Names
Act of Admission or Election

CELEBRATION OF THE CALL
TO CONTINUING CONVERSION

Presentation of the Candidates
Affirmation by the Sponsors [and the Assembly]
Act of Recognition

Intercessions for the Elect and the Candidates
Prayer over the Elect and the Candidates
Dismissal of the Elect

LITURGY OF THE EUCHARIST

4 CELEBRATION AT THE EASTER VIGIL OF THE SACRAMENTS OF INITIATION AND OF THE RITE OF RECEPTION INTO THE FULL COMMUNION OF THE CATHOLIC CHURCH

562   Pastoral considerations may suggest that along with the celebration of the sacraments of Christian initiation the Easter Vigil should include the rite of reception of already baptized Christians into the full communion of the Catholic Church. But such a decision must be guided by the theological and pastoral directives proper to each rite. The model provided here simply arranges the ritual elements belonging to such a combined celebration. But the model can only be used properly in the light of nos. 206–217, regarding celebration of the sacraments of Christian initiation, and of nos. 473–486, regarding the rite of reception into the full communion of the Catholic Church.

563   Inclusion at the Easter Vigil of the rite of reception into full communion may also be opportune liturgically, especially when the candidates have undergone a lengthy period of spiritual formation coinciding with Lent. In the liturgical year the Easter Vigil, the preeminent commemoration of Christ's paschal mystery, is the preferred occasion for the celebration in which the elect will enter the paschal mystery through baptism, confirmation, and eucharist. Candidates for reception, who in baptism have already been justified by faith and incorporated into Christ,[1] are entering fully into a community that is constituted by its communion both in faith and in the sacramental sharing of the paschal mystery. The celebration of their reception at the Easter Vigil provides the candidates with the privileged opportunity to recall and reaffirm their own baptism, "the sacramental bond of unity [and] foundation of communion between all Christians."[2] At the Easter Vigil these candidates can make their profession of faith by joining the community in the renewal of the baptismal promises, and, if they have not yet been confirmed, they can receive the sacrament of confirmation, which is intimately connected with baptism. Since of its nature baptism points to complete

---

[1] See Secretariat for Christian Unity, *Ecumenical Directory I*, no. 11: AAS 59 (1967), 578–579. Vatican Council II, Decree on Ecumenism *Unitatis redintegratio*, no. 3.

[2] See *Ecumenical Directory I*, no. 11: AAS 59 (1967), 578. Vatican Council II, Decree on Ecumenism *Unitatis redintegratio*, no. 22.

entrance into eucharistic communion,[3] the baptismal themes of the Easter Vigil can serve to emphasize why the high point of the candidates' reception is their sharing in the eucharist with the Catholic community for the first time (see no. 475.1).

564 The decision to combine the two celebrations at the Easter Vigil must be guided by the provision in the *Rite of Reception*, Introduction (no. 475.2). The decision should, then, be consistent in the actual situation with respect for ecumenical values and be guided by attentiveness both to local conditions and to personal and family preferences. The person to be received should always be consulted about the form of reception (see no. 475.2).

565 In its actual arrangement the celebration itself must reflect the status of candidates for reception into the full communion of the Catholic Church: such candidates have already been incorporated into Christ in baptism and anything that would equate them with catechumens is to be absolutely avoided (see no. 477).

---

[3] See Vatican Council II, Decree on Ecumenism *Unitatis redintegratio*, no. 22.

OUTLINE OF THE RITE

SERVICE OF LIGHT

LITURGY OF THE WORD

CELEBRATION OF BAPTISM

Presentation of the Candidates for Baptism
Invitation to Prayer
Litany of the Saints
Blessing of the Water
Profession of Faith
   Renunciation of Sin
   Profession of Faith
Baptism
Explanatory Rites
   [Anointing after Baptism]
   [Clothing with a Baptismal Garment]
   Presentation of a Lighted Candle

RENEWAL OF BAPTISMAL PROMISES

Invitation
Renewal of Baptismal Promises
   Renunciation of Sin
   Profession of Faith
Sprinkling with Baptismal Water

114

CELEBRATION OF RECEPTION

Invitation
Profession by the Candidates
Act of Reception

CELEBRATION OF CONFIRMATION

Invitation
Laying on of Hands
Anointing with Chrism

LITURGY OF THE EUCHARIST

NATIONAL STATUTES
FOR THE CATECHUMENATE

NATIONAL STATUTES FOR THE CATECHUMENATE

APPROVED BY THE
NATIONAL CONFERENCE OF CATHOLIC BISHOPS
ON 11 NOVEMBER 1986

Confirmed by the Congregation for Divine Worship on 26 June 1988
(Prot. 1191/86)

PRECATECHUMENATE

1   Any reception or service of welcome or prayer for inquirers at the beginning or during a precatechumenate (or in an earlier period of evangelization) must be entirely informal. Such meetings should take into account that the inquirers are not yet catechumens and that the rite of acceptance into the order of catechumens, intended for those who have been converted from unbelief and have initial faith, may not be anticipated.

CATECHUMENATE

2   The term "catechumen" should be strictly reserved for the unbaptized who have been admitted into the order of catechumens; the term "convert" should be reserved strictly for those converted from unbelief to Christian belief and never used of those baptized Christians who are received into the full communion of the Catholic Church.

3   This holds true even if elements of catechumenal formation are appropriate for those who are not catechumens, namely, (a) baptized Catholic Christians who have not received catechetical instruction and whose Christian initiation has not been completed by confirmation and eucharist and (b) baptized Christians who have been members of another Church or ecclesial community and seek to be received into the full communion of the Catholic Church.

4   If the catechumenal preparation takes place in a non-parochial setting

such as a center, school, or other institution, the catechumens should be introduced into the Christian life of a parish or similar community from the very beginning of the catechumenate, so that after their initiation and mystagogy they will not find themselves isolated from the ordinary life of the Christian people.

5   In the celebration of the rite of acceptance into the order of catechumens, it is for the diocesan bishop to determine whether the additional rites listed in no. 74, *Rite of Christian Initiation of Adults,* are to be incorporated (see no. 33.5).

6   The period of catechumenate, beginning at acceptance into the order of catechumens and including both the catechumenate proper and the period of purification and enlightenment after election or enrollment of names, should extend for at least one year of formation, instruction, and probation. Ordinarily this period should go from at least the Easter season of one year until the next; preferably it should begin before Lent in one year and extend until Easter of the following year.

7   A thoroughly comprehensive catechesis on the truths of Catholic doctrine and moral life, aided by approved catechetical texts, is to be provided during the period of the catechumenate (see RCIA, no. 75).

CATECHUMENS

8   Catechumens should be encouraged to seek blessings and other suffrages from the Church, since they are of the household of Christ; they are entitled to Christian burial should they die before the completion of their initiation.

9   In this case, the funeral liturgy, including the funeral Mass, should be celebrated as usual, omitting only language referring directly to the sacraments which the catechumen has not received. In view of the sensibilities of the immediate family of the deceased catechumen, however, the funeral Mass may be omitted at the discretion of the pastor.

10   The marriages of catechumens, whether with other catechumens or with baptized Christians or even non-Christians, should be celebrated at a liturgy of the word and never at the eucharistic liturgy. Chapter III of the

Rite of Marriage is to be followed, but the nuptial blessing in Chapter I, no. 33, may be used, all references to eucharistic sharing being omitted.

MINISTER OF BAPTISM AND CONFIRMATION

11   The diocesan bishop is the proper minister of the sacraments of initiation for adults, including children of catechetical age, in accord with canon 852:1. If he is unable to celebrate the sacraments of initiation with all the candidates of the local church, he should at least celebrate the rite of election or enrollment of names, ordinarily at the beginning of Lent, for the catechumens of the diocese.

12   Priests who do not exercise a pastoral office but participate in a catechumenal program require a mandate from the diocesan bishop if they are to baptize adults; they then do not require any additional mandate or authorization in order to confirm, but have the faculty to confirm from the law, as do priests who baptize adults in the exercise of their pastoral office.

13   Since those who have the faculty to confirm are bound to exercise it in accord with canon 885:2, and may not be prohibited from using the faculty, a diocesan bishop who is desirous of confirming neophytes should reserve to himself the baptism of adults in accord with canon 863.

CELEBRATION OF THE SACRAMENTS OF INITIATION

14   In order to signify clearly the interrelation or coalescence of the three sacraments which are required for full Christian initiation (canon 842:2), adult candidates, including children of catechetical age, are to receive baptism, confirmation, and eucharist in a single eucharistic celebration, whether at the Easter Vigil or, if necessary, at some other time.

15   Candidates for initiation, as well as those who assist them and participate in the celebration of the Easter Vigil with them, are encouraged to keep and extend the paschal fast of Good Friday, as determined by canon 1251, throughout the day of Holy Saturday until the end of the Vigil itself, in accord with the Constitution on the Liturgy, *Sacrosanctum Concilium,* art. 110.

16   The rite of anointing with the oil of catechumens is to be omitted in the baptism of adults at the Easter Vigil.

17   Baptism by immersion is the fuller and more expressive sign of the sacrament and, therefore, provision should be made for its more frequent use in the baptism of adults. The provision of the *Rite of Christian Initiation of Adults* for partial immersion, namely, immersion of the candidate's head, should be taken into account.

CHILDREN OF CATECHETICAL AGE

18   Since children who have reached the use of reason are considered, for purposes of Christian initiation, to be adults (canon 852:1), their formation should follow the general pattern of the ordinary catechumenate as far as possible, with the appropriate adaptations permitted by the ritual. They should receive the sacraments of baptism, confirmation, and eucharist at the Easter Vigil, together with the older catechumens.

19   Some elements of the ordinary catechetical instruction of baptized children before their reception of the sacraments of confirmation and eucharist may be appropriately shared with catechumens of catechetical age. Their condition and status as catechumens, however, should not be compromised or confused, nor should they receive the sacraments of initiation in any sequence other than that determined in the ritual of Christian initiation.

ABBREVIATED CATECHUMENATE

20   The abbreviated catechumenate, which the diocesan bishop may permit only in individual and exceptional cases, as described in nos. 331–332 of the *Rite of Christian Initiation of Adults,* should always be as limited as possible. It should extend over a substantial and appropriate period of time. The rites prior to sacramental initiation should not be unduly compressed, much less celebrated on a single occasion. The catechumenate of persons who move from one parish to another or from one diocese to another should not on that account alone be abbreviated.

21   Candidates who have received their formation in an abbreviated catechumenate should receive the sacraments of Christian initiation at the Easter

Vigil, if possible, together with candidates who have participated in the more extended catechumenate. They should also participate in the period of mystagogy, to the extent possible.

MYSTAGOGY

22 After the completion of their Christian initiation in the sacraments of baptism, confirmation, and eucharist, the neophytes should begin the period of mystagogy by participating in the principal Sunday eucharist of the community throughout the Easter season, which ends on Pentecost Sunday. They should do this as a body in company with their godparents and those who have assisted in their Christian formation.

23 Under the moderation of the diocesan bishop, the mystagogy should embrace a deepened understanding of the mysteries of baptism, confirmation, and the eucharist, and especially of the eucharist as the continuing celebration of faith and conversion.

24 After the immediate mystagogy or postbaptismal catechesis during the Easter season, the program for the neophytes should extend until the anniversary of Christian initiation, with at least monthly assemblies of the neophytes for their deeper Christian formation and incorporation into the full life of the Christian community.

UNCATECHIZED ADULT CATHOLICS

25 Although baptized adult Catholics who have never received catechetical instruction or been admitted to the sacraments of confirmation and eucharist are not catechumens, some elements of the usual catechumenal formation are appropriate to their preparation for the sacraments, in accord with the norms of the ritual, "Preparation of Uncatechized Adults for Confirmation and Eucharist."

26 Although it is not generally recommended, if the sacramental initiation of such candidates is completed with confirmation and eucharist on the same occasion as the celebration of the full Christian initiation of candidates for baptism, the condition and status of those already baptized should be carefully respected and distinguished.

123

27 The celebration of the sacrament of reconciliation with candidates for confirmation and eucharist is to be carried out at a time prior to and distinct from the celebration of confirmation and the eucharist. As part of the formation of such candidates, they should be encouraged in the frequent celebration of this sacrament.

28 Priests mentioned in canon 883:2 also have the faculty to confirm (a) in the case of the readmission to communion of a baptized Catholic who has been an apostate from the faith and also (b) in the case of a baptized Catholic who has without fault been instructed in a non-Catholic religion or adhered to a non-Catholic religion, but (c) not in the case of a baptized Catholic who without his or her fault never put the faith into practice.

29 In the instance mentioned in no. 28 c, in order to maintain the interrelationship and sequence of confirmation and eucharist as defined in canon 842:2, priests who lack the faculty to confirm should seek it from the diocesan bishop, who may, in accord with canon 884:1, grant the faculty if he judges it necessary.

RECEPTION INTO FULL CATHOLIC COMMUNION

30 Those who have already been baptized in another Church or ecclesial community should not be treated as catechumens or so designated. Their doctrinal and spiritual preparation for reception into full Catholic communion should be determined according to the individual case, that is, it should depend on the extent to which the baptized person has led a Christian life within a community of faith and been appropriately catechized to deepen his or her inner adherence to the Church.

31 Those who have been baptized but have received relatively little Christian upbringing may participate in the elements of catechumenal formation so far as necessary and appropriate, but should not take part in rites intended for the unbaptized catechumens. They may, however, participate in celebrations of the word together with catechumens. In addition they may be included with uncatechized adult Catholics in such rites as may be appropriate among those included or mentioned in the ritual in Part II, 4, "Preparation of Uncatechized Adults for Confirmation and Eucharist." The rites of presentation of the Creed, the Lord's Prayer, and the book of the Gospels

are not proper except for those who have received no Christian instruction and formation. Those baptized persons who have lived as Christians and need only instruction in the Catholic tradition and a degree of probation within the Catholic community should not be asked to undergo a full program parallel to the catechumenate.

32   The reception of candidates into the communion of the Catholic Church should ordinarily take place at the Sunday Eucharist of the parish community, in such a way that it is understood that they are indeed Christian believers who have already shared in the sacramental life of the Church and are now welcomed into the Catholic eucharistic community upon their profession of faith and confirmation, if they have not been confirmed, before receiving the eucharist.

33   It is preferable that reception into full communion not take place at the Easter Vigil lest there be any confusion of such baptized Christians with the candidates for baptism, possible misunderstanding of or even reflection upon the sacrament of baptism celebrated in another Church or ecclesial community, or any perceived triumphalism in the liturgical welcome into the Catholic eucharistic community.

34   Nevertheless if there are both catechumens to be baptized and baptized Christians to be received into full communion at the Vigil, for pastoral reasons and in view of the Vigil's being the principal annual celebration of the Church, the combined rite is to be followed: "Celebration at the Easter Vigil of the Sacraments of Initiation and of the Rite of Reception into the Full Communion of the Catholic Church." A clear distinction should be maintained during the celebration between candidates for sacramental initiation and candidates for reception into full communion, and ecumenical sensitivities should be carefully respected.

35   The "Rite of Reception into the Full Communion of the Catholic Church" respects the traditional sequence of confirmation before eucharist. When the bishop, whose office it is to receive adult Christians into the full communion of the Catholic Church (RCIA, no. 481 [R8]) entrusts the celebration of the rite to a presbyter, the priest receives from the law itself (canon 883:2) the faculty to confirm the candidate for reception and is obliged to use it (canon 885:2); he may not be prohibited from exercising the faculty. The confir-

mation of such candidates for reception should not be deferred, nor should they be admitted to the eucharist until they are confirmed. A diocesan bishop who is desirous of confirming those received into full communion should reserve the rite of reception to himself.

36   The celebration of the sacrament of reconciliation with candidates for reception into full communion is to be carried out at a time prior to and distinct from the celebration of the rite of reception. As part of the formation of such candidates, they should be encouraged in the frequent celebration of this sacrament.

37   There may be a reasonable and prudent doubt concerning the baptism of such Christians which cannot be resolved after serious investigation into the fact and/or validity of baptism, namely, to ascertain whether the person was baptized with water and with the Trinitarian formula, and whether the minister and the recipient of the sacrament had the proper requisite intentions. If conditional baptism then seems necessary, this must be celebrated privately rather than at a public liturgical assembly of the community and with only those limited rites which the diocesan bishop determines. The reception into full communion should take place later at the Sunday Eucharist of the community.

DOCUMENTATION

The *Rite of Christian Initiation of Adults* incorporates the (slight) emendations of the introduction (*praenotanda*) occasioned by the promulgation of the Code of Canon Law in 1983. It does not, however, include the text of pertinent canons or the underlying conciliar decisions and statements on the catechumenate, although the latter are reflected in the introduction to the ritual. In order to have these texts available in one place, this documentary appendix has been compiled.

A. CONCILIAR CONSTITUTIONS AND DECREES

Unless otherwise noted all translations are from: *Documents on the Liturgy, 1963–1979: Conciliar, Papal, and Curial Texts* (Collegeville, MN: The Liturgical Press, 1982)

126

Constitution on the Liturgy *Sacrosanctum Concilium,* art. 64:

The catechumenate for adults, divided into several stages, is to be restored and put into use at the discretion of the local Ordinary. By this means the time of the catechumenate, which is intended as a period of well-suited instruction, may be sanctified by sacred rites to be celebrated at successive intervals of time.

Constitution on the Liturgy *Sacrosanctum Concilium,* art. 65:

With art. 37–40 of this Constitution as the norm, it is lawful in mission lands to allow, besides what is part of Christian tradition, those initiation elements in use among individual peoples, to the extent that such elements are compatible with the Christian rite of initiation.

Constitution on the Liturgy *Sacrosanctum Concilium,* art. 66:

Both of the rites for the baptism of adults are to be revised: not only the simpler rite, but also the more solemn one, with proper attention to the restored catechumenate. A special Mass "On the Occasion of a Baptism" is to be incorporated into the Roman Missal.

Dogmatic Constitution on the Church *Lumen Gentium,* no. 14:

This holy Council first of all turns its attention to the Catholic faithful. Basing itself on scripture and tradition, it teaches that the Church, a pilgrim now on earth, is necessary for salvation: the one Christ is mediator and the way of salvation; he is present to us in his body which is the Church. He himself explicitly asserted the necessity of faith and baptism (see Mark 16:16; John 3:5), and thereby affirmed at the same time the necessity of the Church which men enter through baptism as through a door. Hence they could not be saved who, knowing that the Catholic church was founded as necessary by God through Christ, would refuse either to enter it, or to remain in it.

Fully incorporated into the Church are those who, possessing the Spirit of Christ, accept all the means of salvation given to the Church together with her entire organization, and who—by the bonds constituted by the profession of faith, the sacraments, ecclesiastical government, and communion—are joined in the visible structure of the Church of Christ, who rules her through the Supreme Pontiff and the bishops. Even though incorporated into the Church, one who does not however persevere in charity is not saved. He remains indeed in the bosom of the Church, but "in body" not "in heart." All children of the Church should nevertheless remember that their exalted condition results, not from their own merits, but from the grace of Christ. If they fail to respond in thought, word and deed to that grace, not only shall they not be saved, but they shall be the more severely judged.

Catechumens who, moved by the Holy Spirit, desire with an explicit intention to be incorporated into the Church, are by that very intention joined to her.

With love and solicitude mother Church already embraces them as her own (Flannery translation).

Decree on the Church's Missionary Activity *Ad gentes,* no. 13:

Whenever God opens a door for the word in order to declare the mystery of Christ (see Colossians 4:3) then the living God, and he whom he has sent for the salvation of all, Jesus Christ (see 1 Thessalonians 1:9–10; 1 Corinthians 1:18–21; Galatians 1:31; Acts 14:15–17; 17:22–31), are confidently and perseveringly (see Acts 4:13, 29, 31; 9:27, 28; 13:40; 14:3; 19:8; 26:26; 28:31; 1 Thessalonians 2:2; 2 Corinthians 3:12; 7:4; Philippians 1:20; Ephesians 3:12; 6:19–20) proclaimed (see 1 Corinthians 9:15; Romans 10:14) to all men (see Mark 16:15). And this is in order that non-Christians, whose heart is being opened by the Holy Spirit (see Acts 16:4), might, while believing, freely turn to the Lord who, since he is the "way, the truth and the life" (John 14:6), will satisfy all their inner hopes, or rather infinitely surpass them.

This conversion is, indeed, only initial; sufficient however to make a man realize that he has been snatched from sin, and is being led into the mystery of God's love, who invites him to establish a personal relationship with him in Christ. Under the movement of divine grace the new convert sets out on a spiritual journey by means of which, while already sharing through faith in the mystery of the death and resurrection, he passes from the old man to the new man who has been made perfect in Christ (see Colossians 3:5–10; Ephesians 4:20–24). This transition, which involves a progressive change of outlook and morals, should be manifested in its social implications and effected gradually during the period of catechumenate. Since the Lord in whom he believes is a sign of contradiction (see Luke 2:34; Matthew 10:34–39) the convert often has to suffer misunderstanding and separation, but he also experiences those joys which are generously granted by God.

The Church strictly forbids that anyone should be forced to accept the faith, or be induced or enticed by unworthy devices; as it likewise strongly defends the right that no one should be frightened away from the faith by unjust persecutions. In accordance with the very ancient practice of the Church, the motives for the conversion should be examined and, if necessary, purified (Flannery translation).

Decree on the Church's Missionary Activity *Ad gentes,* no. 14:

Those who through the Church have accepted from the Father faith in Christ should be admitted to the catechumenate by means of liturgical ceremonies. The catechumenate means not simply a presentation of teachings and precepts, but a formation in the whole of Christian life and a sufficiently prolonged period of training; by these means the disciples will become bound to Christ as their master. Catechumens should therefore be properly initiated into the mystery of salvation and the practices of gospel living; by means of sacred rites celebrated at successive times, they should be led gradually into the life of faith, liturgy, and charity belonging to the people of God.

Next, freed from the power of darkness, dying, buried, and risen again together with Christ through the sacraments of Christian initiation, they receive the Spirit of adoption of children, and with the whole people of God celebrate the memorial of the Lord's death and resurrection.

There is a great need for a reform of the Lenten and Easter liturgy so that it will be a spiritual preparation of the catechumens for the celebration of the paschal mystery, the rites of which will include their being reborn to Christ through baptism.

Christian initiation during the catechumenate is not the concern of catechists or priests alone, but of the whole community of believers and especially of god-parents, so that from the outset the catechumens will have a sense of being part of the people of God. Moreover, because the Church's life is apostolic, catechu-mens should learn to take an active share in the evangelization and the building up of the Church through the witness of their life and the profession of their faith.

Finally, the new code of canon law should set out clearly the juridic status of catechumens; they are already joined to the Church, already part of Christ's household, and are in many cases already living a life of faith, hope, and charity.

Decree on the Church's Missionary Activity *Ad gentes,* no. 15:

The Holy Spirit calls all to Christ through the seed of the word and the preaching of the Gospel and inspires in hearts the obedience of faith. When in the womb of the baptismal font the Spirit gives birth into a new life to those who believe in Christ, he gathers them all together into the one people of God, "a chosen race, a royal priesthood, a holy nation, God's own people" (1 Peter 2:9).

As God's co-workers, therefore, missionaries are to create congregations of be-lievers of a kind that, living in a way worthy of their calling, will carry out the divinely appointed offices of priest, prophet, and king. This is how the Christian community becomes a sign of God's presence in the world: by the eucharistic sacrifice it goes constantly with Christ to the Father; strengthened by God's word, it bears witness to Christ; it walks in charity and burns with the apostolic spirit. Right from the beginning the Christian community should be trained to be as far as possible self-sufficient in regard to its own needs.

Decree on the Pastoral Office of Bishops in the Church *Christus Dominus,* no. 14:

[Bishops] should ... take steps toward restoring the instruction of adult cate-chumens or toward adapting it more effectively.

Decree on the Ministry and Life of Priests *Presbyterorum ordinis,* no. 5:

God, who alone is holy and the author of holiness, willed to take to himself as companions and helpers men who would humbly dedicate themselves to the work of making others holy. Through the ministry of the bishop God consecrates priests to be sharers of a special title in the priesthood of Christ. In exercising sacred functions they act therefore as the ministers of him who in the liturgy continually fulfills his priestly office on our behalf by the action of his Spirit. By baptism men and women are brought into the people of God and the Church; by the oil of the sick those who are ill find relief; by the celebration of Mass people sacramentally offer the sacrifice of Christ. But in administering all the sacraments, as St. Ignatius the Martyr already attested in the early days of the Church, priests, on various grounds, are linked hierarchically with their bishop and so, in a certain way, bring his presence to every gathering of the faithful.

The other sacraments, like every ministry of the Church and every work of the apostolate, are linked with the holy eucharist and have it as their end. For the eucharist contains the Church's entire spiritual wealth, that is, Christ, himself. He is our Passover and living bread; through his flesh, made living and life-giving by the Holy Spirit, he is bringing life to people and thereby inviting them to offer themselves together with him, as well as their labors and all created things. The eucharist therefore stands as the source and apex of all evangelization: catechumens are led gradually toward a share in the eucharist and the faithful who already bear the seal of baptism and confirmation enter through the eucharist more fully into the Body of Christ.

Decree on the Ministry and Life of Priests *Presbyterorum ordinis*, no. 6:

The pastor's task is not limited to individual care of the faithful. It extends by right also to the formation of a genuine Christian community. But if a community spirit is to be properly cultivated it must embrace not only the local church but the universal Church. A local community ought not merely to promote the care of the faithful within itself, but should be imbued with the missionary spirit and smooth the path to Christ for all men. But it must regard as its special charge those under instruction and the newly converted who are gradually educated in knowing and living the Christian life (Flannery translation).

B. CODE OF CANON LAW

Translations are from: *Code of Canon Law: Latin—English Edition* (Washington, DC: The Canon Law Society of America, 1983)

206   1. Catechumens are in union with the Church in a special manner, that is, under the influence of the Holy Spirit, they ask to be incorporated into the Church by explicit choice and are therefore united with the Church by that choice just as by a life of faith, hope and charity which they lead the Church already cherishes them as its own.

2. The Church has special care for catechumens; the Church invites them

to lead the evangelical life and introduces them to the celebration of sacred rites, and grants them various prerogatives which are proper to Christians.

1. By the witness of their life and words missionaries are to establish a sincere dialogue with those who do not believe in Christ in order that through methods suited to their characteristics and culture avenues may be open to them by which they can be led to an understanding of the gospel message.

2. Missionaries are to see to it that they teach the truths of faith to those whom they judge to be ready to accept the gospel message so that these persons can be admitted to the reception of baptism when they freely request it.

1. After a period of pre-catechumenate has elapsed, persons who have manifested a willingness to embrace faith in Christ are to be admitted to the catechumenate in liturgical ceremonies and their names are to be registered in a book destined for this purpose.

2. Through instruction and an apprenticeship in the Christian life catechumens are suitably to be initiated into the mystery of salvation and introduced to the life of faith, liturgy, charity of the people of God and the apostolate.

3. It is the responsibility of the conference of bishops to issue statutes by which the catechumenate is regulated; these statutes are to determine what things are to be expected of catechumens and define what prerogatives are recognized as theirs.

Through a suitable instruction neophytes are to be formed to a more thorough understanding of the gospel truth and the baptismal duties to be fulfilled; they are to be imbued with a love of Christ and of His Church.

2. The sacraments of baptism, confirmation, and the Most Holy Eucharist are so interrelated that they are required for full Christian initiation.

1. An adult who intends to receive baptism is to be admitted to the catechumenate and, to the extent possible, be led through the several stages to sacramental initiation, in accord with the order of initiation

adapted by the conference of bishops and the special norms published by it.

852   1. What is prescribed in the canons on the baptism of an adult is applicable to all who are no longer infants but have attained the use of reason.

863   The baptism of adults, at least those who have completed fourteen years of age is to be referred to the bishop so that it may be conferred by him, if he judges it expedient.

865   1. To be baptized, it is required that an adult have manifested the will to receive baptism, be sufficiently instructed in the truths of faith and in Christian obligations and be tested in the Christian life by means of the catechumenate; the adult is also to be exhorted to have sorrow for personal sins.

2. An adult in danger of death may be baptized if, having some knowledge of the principal truths of faith, the person has in any way manifested an intention of receiving baptism and promises to observe the commandments of the Christian religion.

866   Unless a grave reason prevents it, an adult who is baptized is to be confirmed immediately after baptism and participate in the celebration of the Eucharist, also receiving Communion.

869   1. If there is a doubt whether one has been baptized or whether baptism was validly conferred and the doubt remains after serious investigation, baptism is to be conferred conditionally.

2. Those baptized in a non-Catholic ecclesial community are not to be baptized conditionally unless, after an examination of the matter and the form of words used in the conferral of baptism and after a consideration of the intention of an adult baptized person and of the minister of the baptism, a serious reason for doubting the validity of the baptism is present.

3. If the conferral or the validity of the baptism in the cases mentioned in nos. 1 and 2 remains doubtful, baptism is not to be conferred until the doctrine of the sacrament of baptism is explained to the person, if an adult, and the reasons for the doubtful validity of the baptism have been explained to the adult recipient or, in the case of an infant, to the parents.

The following have the faculty of administering confirmation by the law itself:

1. within the limits of their territory, those who are equivalent in law to the diocesan bishop;

2. with regard to the person in question, the presbyter who by reason of office or mandate of the diocesan bishop baptizes one who is no longer an infant or one already baptized whom he admits into the full communion of the Catholic Church;

3. with regard to those in danger of death, the pastor or indeed any presbyter.

1. The diocesan bishop is to administer confirmation personally or see that it is administered by another bishop, but if necessity requires he may give the faculty to administer this sacrament to one or more specified presbyters.

2. For a grave cause, a bishop and likewise a presbyter who has the faculty to confirm by virtue of law or special concession of competent authority may in individual cases associate presbyters with themselves so that they may administer the sacrament.

3. A presbyter who has this faculty must use it for those in whose favor the faculty was granted.

Blessings, to be imparted especially to Catholics, can also be given to catechumens and even to non-Catholics unless a church prohibition precludes this.

1. As regards funeral rites catechumens are to be considered members of the Christian faithful.

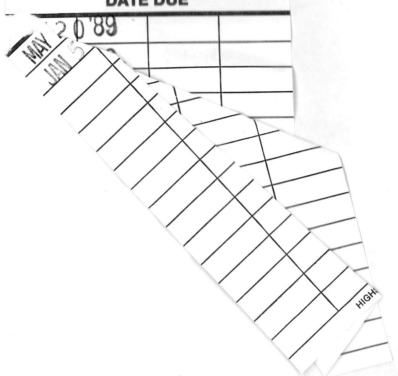

DATE DUE

MAY 2 0 '89

JAN 5

HIGH